# Not Even God
## The Curious Partnership of God and Man

by Bryan Rocine

B & J
Boaz & Jachin Publishing
DeWitt, NY

**Not Even God:**
**The Curious Partnership of God and Man**
by Bryan Rocine

www.NotEvenGod.com

Published by
Boaz and Jachin Publishing
PO Box 183
DeWitt, NY 13214

International Standard Book Number:
978-0-9820702-0-8

*Printed in the United States of America*

For
Isaiah, Bethany, Jeremy, and Cori.

*I have no greater joy than to hear that my children
are walking in the truth.*
3 John 1:4

3

*What [God] is watching and waiting and working for is something that is not easy even for God, because, from the nature of the case, even He cannot produce it by a mere act of power. He is waiting and watching for it both in Miss Bates and in Dick Firkin. It is something they can freely give Him or freely refuse Him. Will they, or will they not, turn to Him and thus fulfill the only purpose for which they were created? Their free will is trembling inside them like a needle of a compass. But this is a needle that can choose. It can point to its true North; but it need not. Will the needle swing round, and settle, and point to God? He can help it to do so. He cannot force it.*

--C. S. Lewis, *Mere Christianity*,
(HarperSanFrancisco, 2001), 211-212.

# CONTENTS

# Introduction

Apparently, not even God can have it all.

The Sunday school teachers at the neighborhood church may bristle at the thought that the Lord endures limits of any sort. After all, "God can do anything," is part of the believer's pledge of allegiance. And for a lot of people the thought of God doing *anything* means that God can have *everything*.

But if I check against the pit of my gut instead of parroting the "party line," my own circle of friends suggests the Lord must be putting up with something or someone. God must be *tolerating*. For instance, the twenty-one year old son of one friend died in a car wreck; another friend, a mother of three, got cancer; and one of my dearest friends, a father of four, was murdered. Would it be irreverent if a pastor of twenty-plus years asks if the Almighty suffered a little along with my friends?

To me, suffering means tolerating in the senses of both permitting and enduring. And suppose God is tolerating. Why would God tolerate anything if tolerating weren't in some way required of him? Of course, "requirements" for a sovereign God aren't part of the typical Sunday school lesson either.

Back to my three friends. All of them belong to (or in the case of my deceased friend, read past tense) the congregation of which I am a pastor, and all three had faith in the goodness of God in spite of their trials. In the chapters that follow, we will consider their stories and others to explore the idea that God doesn't always get what he wants but how he may if we work with him. The stories are not all sad. On the contrary, some of them are gloriously happy. I think what they have in common is that they are all helpful for exploring the curious partnership of God and man in our troubled world. When it comes to thinking about God, most of our days offer no cause for alarm because most of us wake up healthy, do our business or play our games without major tragedy, and get along at least reasonably well with our loved ones, co-workers, and neighbors. Our pleasant, affirming, or at least bearable experiences usually outnumber the disturbing events of our lives and lull us into a sort of mental at-ease. On the other hand, even one ordeal, our own or someone else's, can weigh so heavily on our minds it can make us forget about the happier times. Incidents of injustice, sickness, and disaster, though so much fewer in number than the happy stories, can ruin our peace.

Trouble wakes us up to some big questions. We believe that if God is God, he must be good, so how can there be so much evil and suffering in his world? If God is God, he is all-powerful, so why doesn't he just snap his fingers and put an end to all the evil? When the primordial world was in darkness he only had to proclaim, "Let there be light!" and there it was. He should just sort of do it again, commanding, "Let there be good!" or "Let there be peace!" If God is God, why did he even create a world in which evil is allowed? As we try to understand the Lord, trouble in our world may leave us in a quandary.

Maybe we wonder for nothing. Maybe the world only *looks* troubled. Maybe God has it in his perfect and absolute control at all times, and we simply don't appreciate what we are looking at. Perhaps we're just not smart enough to behold the beauty beneath the mess. We will just have to wait until we hear the moral of the story.

Hardly. When the really cruel happens—Holocausts, 9/11's, tsunamis in Indonesia, children starving, HIV/AIDS, a shooting rampage on school grounds—the wondering-for-nothing explanation is impossible to swallow. If such senseless evil happening to decent people is God's idea of control, then we don't like it. And what about when we are not merely reading about devastation in the newspaper, but it intrudes into our own homes, especially when someone dear to us suffers? We may find ourselves starting to squirm in our seats while we wonder. We want answers.

The difficulty of trying to explain how evil and suffering can co-exist with a sovereign God has been a concern for generations of theologians and philosophers. Stacks of their books and articles have discussed this issue with careful, logical arguments about the workings of the ultimate realities. The daunting list of subject headings includes, for example, Calvinism, Arminianism, Molinism; simple foreknowledge, middle knowledge, divine nescience; soteriology, theodicy, and hermeneutics. The trouble is that the arguments sometimes sound more like legalese or geometry proofs than faith-talk.

An occasional visit to the CNN website will incite about as many *why's* to ask God as a visit to the theology section of a university library. A scan of *Time* magazine will bring the theologian's questions down from the ivory towers to the ditches. In other words, modern media ensures that common folk, like philosophers, will wrestle with and care about why there is so much trouble in God's ever-shrinking world, even though they are not trained in theology as a special discipline. Hard times do not mean common people can be expected to become Ph.D.'s, Th.D.'s, or D.Div.'s in order to get answers. Neither does a lack of formal training mean that lay people will live happily in their ignorance.

So what are we supposed to think about God?

Maybe God is *not* in control. (Excuse me if I sometimes sound like I am thinking out loud in this book.) I mean, maybe he is in control somewhere at the top of it all, like the CEO of the largest corporation ever. But maybe he is holed up in the executive suite on the top floor while we laborers are down at street level running our own hit-and-miss show. Any large company *will* run a haphazard and wasteful course if the lower and higher levels of the corporate structure aren't networking. Maybe the Great CEO of heaven is displeased with how bankrupt his creation sometimes is, maybe even more displeased than we are. But have we and the Lord been isolated in our separate departments by some irresistible cosmic management structure? Or are we talking?

It was God who gave us these very busy minds of ours. If so, it doesn't seem as though we should have to endure pain in the Lord's world with a blind salute as passive heroes. No doubt, the Divine Purpose is more complex and far-reaching than we will ever fully grasp with our limited intellects. At times we may simply have to trust rather than understand, but even the Lord invites us in the Bible to enter into a dialectic: *"Come let us reason together."** A patriarch of the faith, Abraham, questioned the Lord's integrity: *"Will not the Judge of all the earth do right?"*† At least in Abraham's case, the Lord thought it was a fair question. I think he has some answers for us, too.

I hope it's not surprising that the Bible, written especially for the common man, offers help and compassion. Page after page of the Bible, like the world we live in, contains a share of trouble. In it some bad people get rich and a lot of good people get hurt. Suitable to honesty, it portrays life in its messiest inconsistencies. So like us, the Bible's writers sometimes wrestle with the co-existence of grief and a sovereign God. And sometimes they provide some inspired resolutions that still sing with eloquence and relevance. To pursue the first purpose of this book, finding peace with the Lord in an often-upsetting world, we will take a fresh look at

---

* Isaiah 1:8. All quotes from the Bible will be in italics and from the New International Version unless otherwise noted.
† Genesis 18:25.

some familiar Bible passages, and perhaps a first look at some unfamiliar. Another of this book's purposes is to encourage a vital relationship with God. Inspiration comes from an intriguing statement in the Bible: ...*we are God's fellow workers.*[*] We might call it collaboration. In a sense, God will allow us to write the stories of our lives together with him.

To learn about the curious nature of God's fragile collaboration or partnership with man, we will think about some passages from the Bible and, as mentioned above, numerous stories about some of my friends who learned about this partnership for themselves. A connecting thread will emerge in many of the stories highlighting the important role of prayer. My friends' stories, both the sad and the happy ones, may serve as an encouragement for all of us to live out our own collaboration with the author of life often beginning with a life-changing time of prayer. The answers to prayer are even better than the prayer itself!

One more purpose of this book's combination of Bible commentaries and personal narratives is to encourage its readers to keep trying to find God's will for their lives. Finding and living in the will of God does not often come easily, and hardly ever does it come without somehow surrendering ourselves. We will see that life in the will of God is the blessing worth struggling for. There is indeed a way to think and live that expresses partnership with the loving and living Lord. The Lord can work with humble, typical people and thereby transform their lives.

The personal narratives in this book are all about my "church family." I minister to them and with them at Living Word Church in Syracuse, NY. I have chosen to limit myself to stories about people who are all from one church for a couple of reasons, one being that my friends are "there." In other words, they are my "neighbors." The Bible teaches us

---

[*] 1 Corinthians 3:9.

that we have a special commitment to the neighborhood in which God has placed us, and I want the book to have a feeling of neighborhood and family. I am praying that the readers will feel connected to my friends, who are probably a lot like people they already know. I hope the reader will even see themselves in these stories.

Another reason to stay within my "church family" for this book is to be fair. It doesn't seem quite fair to search the world over for exceptional anecdotes, which will prove the existence of a certain kind of God. Instead, all the stories in this book come from one medium-sized church. The stories are instructive, but there is no reason to consider them exceptional. I certainly do not believe that the Lord's love for my friends and me is any greater than his love for anyone else. If many poignant stories can all come from only one pastor's circle of friends, maybe that will suggest that the Lord himself has a very special interest in you, too.

I must say that writing this book has changed me in ways that I did not anticipate. I began determined to honor the Lord, but as the interviewing process continued I also grew increasingly resolved to give due respect to my friends. During the interviews my friends had all the time they wanted, usually many hours, to recall, retell, and in some cases emotionally re-live their stories. I guess it's not often that any of us are afforded such a luxury, so they all wanted to take advantage! First, their courage impressed me. Not every detail of their lives was complimentary, not all the details made them out as heroes, and a lot of the details were very painful to recall; yet in every case, my friends overcame their discomfort with a common drive. They expressed this drive independently but unanimously—the desire that the Lord would use their experiences to help someone else who wants to believe.

Next, I saw their generosity. They all realized I wasn't writing a book about anyone of them in particular. In other words, none of them would be the star of the show. Rather, I would, in a sense, use them to illustrate a point. None minded being used in this way. My friends encouraged me to choose which details were relevant. They were satisfied for me to pack the details of their lives into a few pages. They seemed to hold in common the motto: "Use it as you will." Their generosity made me feel small and put the pressure on. I pray that I have met their courage and trust with a worthy message and fitting eloquence.

NOT EVEN GOD

# PART I: FREEDOM

## --The Unavoidable Condition
## for God's Project of Love

## CHAPTER ONE

# The Grieving Mother

*Matthew 6:9-10   "This, then, is how you should pray: 'Our Father in heaven, hallowed be your name, your kingdom come, your will be done on earth as it is in heaven.'"*

Jesus was so impressive when in prayer that his followers asked if he could teach them how to pray. As Jewish men, the disciples had already seen more than their share of praying in their homes, in synagogues, at community events, and during their yearly visits to the great Temple in Jerusalem. They had themselves been called on to pray many times. But when they saw Jesus pray, it made them feel almost like they had never prayed before.

What was it? Did Jesus pray more loudly or sway more vigorously than they did? Did he squish his eyes shut until his brows clenched into little fists of intensity? Did he pray so energetically or for so long that everyone else had long since flopped back like they had just finished college entrance exams?

Whatever impressed the disciples, Jesus seemed more than happy to teach them, and the passage from Matthew 6 is part of his lesson. In fact, even though a lot of people call this part of the lesson "The Lord's Prayer," it's even better to understand it as "The Model Prayer," an instructive example.

The entire lesson included points about the proper attitudes and place of prayer. In our Bible passage for this chapter, Jesus taught them about the proper *content* of prayer, that is, about a way of thinking that is appropriate for prayer.

First off, we can consider what it means to pray because it's in prayer that we often start to become God's partners. When we realize that praying is part of a partnership with the Almighty, we may be much more likely to view prayer as the blessing that it's meant to be, rather than a form of penance.

The word, *pray*, simply means, "to ask God." So simply by entering into prayer we should be acknowledging that we are needy and our heavenly Father has the supply. I guess it shouldn't be hard to admit that we need to team up with God more than he needs to team up with us! Prayer expresses our faith that the Father cares and doesn't want us to be without the things we need to do his will. We pray because we believe asking and seeking will really help.

Day one, lesson one on collaborating with God: ask the Father for his kingdom to come, and for his will to be done. "Have your way, Lord Father."

We all probably embrace the concept that the Father's kingdom and will are good things to strive for in prayer. But do we realize such prayer-goals come with a flip-side? Do we realize why Jesus teaches us to pray this way? The request, "May your kingdom come," recognizes the Father's rule over this world is not always respected. "May your will be done," recognizes his will is *not* always done.

Put simply, Jesus wants us to acknowledge that the Lord does not always get his way. He may be dutifully obeyed on the golden streets of heaven, but not always on this grimy earth. Why else would we have to pray for the Father's will to be done? Acknowledging that the Lord does not always have his way is part of the good thinking that Jesus teaches us to do while we pray. Then we can more effectively participate and contribute in prayer to making the world more like heaven.

There is often a terrible moment prior to salvation, and sometimes prior to spiritual growth, when we must admit that we are a mess. It's like remodeling the bathroom. As we uncover all of the room's crookedness and rot, the project can get a lot uglier before it gets bright and straight and clean. More than once I have removed an old wall panel during a bathroom-remodeling project and been hit in the face by the dank, pungent smell of black mold. Ugh! It's not time to put the panel back. It's time to keep digging for the rest of the problem.

When it comes to fixing up our souls, the ugliness is actually humiliating! But for our souls to become healthy, we must first get our arms around the fact that the Lord up in heaven is not having his way with us down here where we are sagging, crooked, or offensive.

To admit our problems seems not only to humiliate us; it seems to diminish God's glory. It's like telling the great Creator up there that his work down here is faulted. Yet the Lord is not One to turn a blind eye to failure or to whitewash a corrupted core. Jesus assures us that we can come to our loving heavenly Father with the most terrible of admissions. Since it means that more of his will can be done in the future, the Father is not opposed to it when we admit that his will is not being done at present.

A certain kind of comfort comes with the common belief of many Christians that God always has his way, and that he is always in control, managing every detail of our lives according to his purposes. It's flattering. It takes the pressure off us. In fact, we may become passive while we repeat our popular Christian mantra, "He makes everything beautiful in his time." More important than feeling comfortable or flattered, however, is asking the question: Is it true that God always has his way? If not, our traditional beliefs will be like a house of cards when the winds of trial come. This book will attempt to show that if we read the Bible without prejudice, we will find that the Bible actually contradicts the common notion of a God who is always having his way.

As another example, Jesus said of his beloved Jerusalem, *"How often I have longed to gather your children together, as a hen gathers her chicks under her wings, but you were not willing."*[*] If we can generalize from this example, it would seem that the Lord wants to protect and nourish us, but he sometimes cannot due to our choices. He is pained by our rebellion and the restraints that rebellion puts on his love. How far can our stubbornness go in thwarting the good will of God? To what extreme has man's rebellion altered the course of human history?

As uncomfortable as it may be, we can use mankind's ugliest descents into violence as a case in the extreme. For instance, there have been at least these seven cases of genocide in the last hundred years:

- The Armenians of Turkey (1915-1918, 1,500,000 dead).
- Stalin's Forced Famine (1932-1933, 7,000,000 dead).
- The Nazi Holocaust (1938-1945, 6,000,000 dead).
- Cambodia (1975-1979, 2,000,000 dead).
- The Kurds of Iraq (1987-1988, 180,000 dead).
- Rwanda (1994, 800,000 dead)
- Bosnia Herzegovina (1992-1995, 200,000 dead).

It's beyond me to imagine God's planning or ordering or preferring nearly 18 million murders. Milosevic, Bashir, Hussein, Pol Pot, Hitler, Stalin—the God who would use such hardened monsters as his instruments would have to be himself the greatest monster of all. Some people believe human

---

[*] Matthew 23:7.

monsters are right now committing genocide against the tribes of the Darfur region of Sudan. It is not God's will.

It's easy to think of other cases of regrettable, horrific violence—for instance, the Bomb. In August of 1945, atomic weapons killed over 200,000 Japanese, mostly women, children, the aged, and infirm, when the US dropped "Little Boy" on Hiroshima and "Fat Man" on Nagasaki. In those horrific moments God did not force open the bomb bay doors of the B-29's. God did not ride the Bomb like a psychotic cavalryman, hooting all the way as it fell to its target. On the contrary, Robert Oppenheimer, director of the Manhattan Project that produced the Bomb, admitted two years later in a lecture at MIT, "...the physicists have known sin; and this is a sin which they cannot lose." We would do best to wonder whether the Lord viewed one of the great horrors of the twentieth century the same way he did when Noah's world filled with violence: *The Lord was grieved that he had made man on the earth, and his heart was filled with pain.**

How can a loving God allow such things? First, we can rest assured they are positively not the efforts of Providence to teach his children hard lessons. Granted, we should learn important lessons from these horrors. Granted, the Lord himself provides us a powerful moral lens through which to view history. But neither our learning nor the Lord's instructive viewpoint proves that the Lord sent the atrocities as our teachers. If God were intentionally sending these scourges to us to teach us, the cost of their lessons would be absurdly unjust. What noble person would want the lessons? Any noble person would gladly forfeit all learning and, most probably, his very life to eliminate one such atrocity. Even in view of the after-life, an eternity in which the Lord promises to make right all the injustices done on this earth, we should never imagine that God, in the name of a lesson, would treat our present suffering with such disregard. We cannot dismiss the atrocities

---

* Genesis 6:6.

of this world, plied by people in rebellion against God, with a cliché: "He makes everything beautiful in its time."
When evil in the world challenges our faith from some distance, for instance in history texts or on the nightly news, playing the philosopher may be a bearable exercise. But when faith and evil meet within the context of our own life's experience, the collision can be insufferable. For instance, Elie Wiesel, in his book *Night*, gives the most eloquent expression of anguish that I have ever encountered in print. He laments his first night at the brink of a Nazi cremation pit as a teenager in 1944:

> Never shall I forget those flames that consumed my
> faith forever.
> Never shall I forget the nocturnal silence that
> deprived me for all eternity of the desire to live.
> Never shall I forget those moments that murdered
> my God and my soul and turned my dreams to
> ashes.
> Never shall I forget those things, even were I
> condemned to live as long as God himself.
> Never.[*]

We understand intellectually what "consumed" Elie's faith that night. His eyes and ears imbibed a reality so harsh his faith could not fathom God would allow it. The inescapable conclusion, as if logic even mattered any more, was that God had been murdered. We can't be so cold as to say Elie ought not to have resorted to such an impious exaggeration. Who knows if we could have spiritually survived such a crisis of faith as well as Elie's memoir indicates he did? On the other hand, this book has just begun to explore why God is worthy of our trust in spite of the evil that is in this world. For one thing,

---

[*] Elie Wiesel, *Night*, (NY: Hill and Wang) 34.

(as Elie Wiesel has eloquently and poetically expresses in his lament) the evil hurts God, too. He didn't want it to be this way.

We will continue a fuller explanation as we proceed chapter by chapter. At this point, as in each coming chapter, we will turn to a story about one of my church friends that may help. This chapter's dear friend, like Elie Wiesel, had to confront evil in such a way that she will never forget it.

One July day in the still, dark hours of the early morning, Nila received the phone call that every parent dreads. On the other end of the line an estranged relative was screaming that Nila's son had died in a ditch, the result of a car wreck. Still in the fog of sleep and not trusting the phone account, Nila called the local hospital. Her son was indeed there. She needed to come right away. That's all they were willing to tell her.

At the hospital it took some time for the concept to penetrate—my son Joe is dead. First Nila heard the moaning of grief. Then she saw the swollen eyes of others at the hospital, her sister and Joe's girlfriend's mother. The hall became a gauntlet of gentle touches on the arm and that too-careful tone of voice as people directed her way. Bright fluorescent lights seemed to wash away all privacy. A doctor approached and inquired whether Nila was Joe's mother. "I'm sorry. Joe didn't make it," Nila remembers him saying. But remembering it now doesn't mean she was absorbing it at the time.

Praying all the while, she approached a man's remains on a gurney. The black jeans and the t-shirt could be Joe's. She told the nurse that was holding her by the elbow, "It's not my son. My son's eyes were green, not brown." The nurse explained why they were brown.

For Nila the proof positive lay in a hand-sized flap of torn t-shirt that lay upside-down. If she turned it over and found a picture of Spider-Man, she would know the dead man was her son. She hesitated. She had given Joe the t-shirt one week before for his twenty-first birthday because Nila knew how her son loved to draw comic book heroes. He would copy some of the classics like Spidey, but his best drawings were originals. Joe was such a gifted artist and such an adventure-loving kid. Everyone liked him for it. Oh, Joe, you and your adventures! Nila turned over the flap—the lithe pose, the red and blue suit, the mirror-like eyes—there was Spider-Man. Joey was really gone.

Bit by bit, people told Nila the details of Joe's death. Joe had been in the back seat of a car driven by a drunken man. When the car collided with a truck broadside, Joe was ejected through the windshield and landed in a ditch. The driver and another passenger squirmed out of the car and left the scene, but the police later apprehended them both. The driver was charged with vehicular manslaughter, the passenger with leaving the scene of an accident. Nila never found out who called the rescue squads that tried for an hour to keep her son alive.

Nila was to fight a noble battle with her grief. In the first week following her son's death she found support in the presence of her church family and recalls how her brothers and sisters in Christ each took on a role in a beautiful patchwork of grace. When she asked me to officiate at her son's funeral, she bravely requested that I reach out to the mourners with the hopeful message of salvation through Jesus. She wanted the Lord to salvage something out of this wreck. She prayed the Gospel message would exert the power of hope and order on the tragedy.

The funeral home was packed with a lot of people that were part of Nila's life before she became a Christian, what we Christians sometimes call our "lives B.C." (Before Christ). It was the same rough crowd that nourished the culture of excess that killed Nila's son. Christians were the outsiders to them, the "holier-than-thou's," so they resented us. And anyone could grant that the appearance of the crowd was not typical in a religious service—homemade tattoos, face-piercings (some years before they became common), thickly painted faces, dirty jeans, t-shirts, and halter-tops. A lot of foreheads were creased, but not with pain or grief. To me the faces looked defiant and angry. Eyes glared. I was shaky, but I didn't want to disappoint the Lord or Nila. I had something to say and began after a deep breath.

After eulogizing Joe, I read to the packed-out funeral home: *"This, then, is how you should pray: '...Your will be done on earth as it is in heaven.'"* I said that we have to pray for God's will to be done on the earth because it's *not* done often enough. Then I became plain: "Joe's death was not God's will. God didn't 'take him,' as some might say. In fact, God had much richer intentions for this promising young man. But alcohol abuse and bad choices have spoiled the purposes of the heavenly Father for this young man. We need to start praying that God's will would be done for a change. We need to start *doing* God's will for a change."

One angry woman muttered to a couple of her cronies and walked out. The rest of the people were still. Heads went down. Foreheads smoothed. A few would even approach me later in the day because they wanted me to pray with them. In the front row at the funeral home, Nila nodded and whispered "Amen." Her faith so impressed me.

Nila tells of a strange experience when she was by the open casket for the last time to say farewell to Joe. As she reached out to put her hand on her son's chest an impression, like a "Stop!" intruded almost like there was a force field prohibiting her. She kept her distance respectfully and thought. "Joe is not mine any more. It's like he was on loan. Loan over."

Whether the event by the casket foreshadowed Nila's coming struggle with grief or not, the struggle came mightily. Nila was to have bouts with depression, sleeplessness, and the aggravation of painful physical symptoms for many months as she grieved. In the end, interpreting the force field at the casket didn't matter because relief would come like a gift one night.

Following her son's death, Nila would sometimes pour out her grief during her private time of prayer. She lamented before the Lord that she had not done more for Joe because her son had died alone in a ditch. She so wished she had been there to comfort him while he took his last breath. To let the Lord know she was still hurting, she would cry and actually stretch out her arms, as if toward the son she could no longer touch. She had become like David in the Bible who also lost his son and poured his grief before the Lord, *"O my son Absalom! O Absalom, my son, my son!"*[*]

On a particular night like this the Lord spoke to her: "My arms are stretching out to many." That's all. It was a familiar image to Nila because it's often celebrated in the Bible, like in Psalm 136:12: *...with a mighty hand and outstretched arm; his love endures forever.*

In a moment the image of the Lord's arms encapsulated for Nila the Lord's cosmic project of love. "My arms are stretching out to many." The arms represented his loving intentions, not only for her and Joe, but also for all people in all time and every place. His dedication to his project of love never tires or weakens. He never stops desiring to rescue the sinful, the lost, and the failing. The Lord was telling her she wasn't the only one who was experiencing a terrible, needless loss. The Lord himself understood her grief because he too feels grief except multiplied as many times over as can be experienced by God alone. There are so many people the Lord wants to touch, but they won't let him.

Nila never grieved that way again. In fact, she was about to have her own chance to be like the Lord's hands reaching out to a lost world.

---

[*] 2 Samuel 18:33.

In the spring after Joe's death, Nila received a letter from the county court inviting her to the sentencing of the man who had been driving when her son was killed. He was guilty of second-degree vehicular manslaughter, and Nila could write the judge a statement and appear in court for the sentencing in two days. She felt she ought to write something, but she was confused as she sat at her kitchen table in front of a blank sheet of paper.

Some things she was hearing about the convicted man were disturbing her. The D. A. reported that the man was remorseless. The driver apparently considered what happened that night to be no more than an unfortunate accident. She heard from others that he had been seen bar-hopping while he was out on bail. How long would it be before the man killed someone else? She felt it was her motherly and civic duty to impress the judge with the weightiness of the case. She prayed while she wrote and thought: "Have your way, this time, Lord. Move me, Lord. Help me have the right words."

Nila entered the courtroom two days later, statement in hand, expecting a court official might accept her letter as an official submission into the court records. She sat in the front row without a clue as to how the proceedings would unfold. People began to fill the chairs. She saw a third grade class come in, apparently on a field trip, and the teacher doing what she could to still them. Next six or seven prisoners dressed in orange jumpsuits shuffled in with a rattle because of their waist and ankle shackles. She wondered which one was Joe's driver without realizing he was actually in plain clothes sitting in the chair right behind her the entire time. The D. A. nodded a greeting to her.

As the last of the court officials took their places, the judge was introduced, and the entire room rustled to its feet for a moment and then settled back down after the judge sat. Behind the judge the room seemed majestic with its massive stone cornices and heavy wood paneling. When the morning sun gleamed through the large windows to the side, Nila thought it was like the "light of God" shining into the room. This room was the last place someone would want to try hiding from justice, she thought. The chatter continuing to emanate from every section of the room seemed disrespectful to her.

Distracted by her private thoughts, Nila was jolted awake when the judge's secretary announced her case. Before she had a chance to hesitate, the D. A. escorted Nila to the middle of the courtroom facing the judge's bench. At the same time another lawyer brought her son's killer to a nearby table. Nila noticed the man's wife and young child had been sitting behind her, too. The judge took over. In official language he said he would be sentencing the convicted man that day, and the victim's mother had a statement. He invited Nila to speak.

This had all happened way too fast! She thought she would just be handing her statement to a court official. The D. A. whispered to her to read her letter. As the paper shook in her hand, the judge encouraged her to take all the time she needed. She folded the letter and put it to her side. The score of private little conversations going on here and there in the big room ceased. Even the third graders hushed.

Nila gave her loss perspective by measuring it against the convict's prison time: "This man is about to be separated from his family for a long time. I am sure he will miss them every moment. But the choices he made nine months ago mean that I will never see my son again no matter how much I miss him." Nila showed the judge a photo of Joe and her with her arm around him. "What happened was not a mere accident. This man chose to get behind the wheel of a car while under the influence of alcohol. It was a choice, not an accident. It was a deadly choice. Now my twenty-one year old son is gone."

She wasn't done. Nila was about to do what Nila does. She was about to do what faith does; it overcomes evil with good. She started thinking about the third graders behind her, the other convicts, the attorneys, everyone in the room. She glanced at the convicted man almost beside her, to her left. He looked forlorn.

"I am not looking for vengeance today. That's not my heart's desire. I don't hate this man, and I am not here to point fingers. I used to abuse alcohol. I have made a lot of wrong choices. I hope the children in this room today will spare themselves trouble and grief and punishment by doing better than I did as a young person. But when I was twenty-one like my son, I gave my life to Jesus Christ. He forgave me and granted me a new chance; I was born again. I want to say to this man that even though he faces a very difficult time of separation from his loved ones, another judgment is coming, a judgment that is forever, when we will give our accounts to the Judge of Heaven. I pray he will take *this* day as a chance to get ready for *that* day." Nila faced the guilty man. "Jesus saved me. He can save you."

For a few moments everyone in the room was frozen, absorbed in respect. Even the judge's eyes had been riveted on Nila as she spoke. A few moments after she finished, everyone began breathing again, and the judge leaned back in his chair. He addressed the guilty man: "Sir, I admonish you to never forget the words of this grieving mother today. I know I never will."

The next day, the headline of a news article read, "Mother's Plea: Salvation, Not Vengeance." The headline confirmed that Nila's faith more than endured a crisis of grief. She overcame grief to become the Lord's outstretched arm in his project of love. In other words, by collaborating with the Lord, Nila not only found relief. She found purpose. She and the Lord were writing the story of her life together.

## CHAPTER TWO

# In the Garden Alone

*Luke 22:42 "Father, if you are willing, take this cup from me; yet not my will, but yours be done."*

Earlier, at his disciples' request, Jesus taught them to pray, "*Your will be done.*" Here Jesus follows his own advice. One could never say of the teacher Jesus, "Do as he says, not as he does."

In fact, the Gospels of Matthew and Mark also record this event, both specifying that Jesus prayed this same way three times. My will; yours. My will; yours. My will, yours— it was not a matter of pulling petals off a daisy. Rather, the repetition expressed a fight. Jesus had freedom to choose, freedom to either cooperate or innovate. He had the freedom to refuse. The battle was so intense that Jesus' blood pressure skyrocketed; as Luke describes it, Jesus' sweat *was like drops of blood falling to the ground.*[*]

Jesus seemed so like us that night as he hesitated at a fork in the road of his life. Straight ahead, the Father's will. Off to the side, his own.

Jesus was not in a university lecture hall expounding on a theology. He was not in a church auditorium preaching under the weight of public accountability. He was in a garden. It was very dark. He asked a few close friends to join him in prayer, but he moved a stone's throw away from even them to

---

[*] Luke 22:44.

be more alone. It's in just such private times of inner struggle that a man's personal beliefs about the workings of the world really come to the surface. You'll really know a person's theology when you see him alone in a trial.

This is not to say that the private Jesus was any different than the public Jesus. On the other hand, the Bible here puts the emphasis on his private self. Maybe the scene in the garden is best viewed as a picture of Jesus' human self and human faith in contrast to his God-ness. What did the Son of Man *really* believe, not in public, but in private? Two things.

First, destiny. Jesus believed to the core that God the Father had a pre-determined plan for his life. It was clear to Jesus what was ahead for him if he cooperated with that plan. The "cup" he was asking the Father to reconsider included arrest, abandonment, an unjust trial, mockery, torture, and ultimately, death. He knew he was destined for crucifixion as *the Lamb of God, who takes away the sin of the world.*\* He would not be climbing down from the cross on his own. Hopefully, someone would remember him fondly enough to take down his dead body from the cross and put it in a grave. This destiny of death was the straight-ahead *yours* of *not my will but yours.*

But second, Jesus also believed fundamentally that it was possible for the Father to adjust his destiny. When Jesus said, *If you are willing, take this cup from me,* he was requesting the Father to save mankind in another way that would be less painful. Ultimately, Jesus accepted that it was imperative to embrace the Father's plan as it was, including the terrible cross. But Jesus' obedience to the plan doesn't eliminate the glimpse we get of his faith that a change in his destiny was, if not a better choice, at least a possibility. If Jesus, in the garden, wasn't just venting or putting on an act of distress in the face of a future that was really a foregone conclusion—if we see his prayer as sincere—he must have

---

\* John 1:29.

believed that God could change his future even in those last few hours. In other words, Jesus was in the same battle of will that any person experiences before he chooses the heavenly Father's plan for his life.

It seems like the human thing to do, to stall while our idea for our lives competes inside us with the Lord's plan. Our will so often makes better sense to us, but that doesn't always mean our plan agrees with the Lord's plan for our lives. Pastor Robert Mazur (or "Brother Bob" as we affectionately call him in the church), the founding pastor of the Living Word Church in Syracuse, NY, felt just this kind of inner struggle between his ideas about how best to serve the Lord and the Lord's plans for Central New York. It's no wonder that Bother Bob's favorite hymn is "In the Garden Alone."

In his first years as a Christian, Brother Bob had ideas of becoming a traveling evangelist. He was good at meeting new people, traveling, reading a crowd. He could boldly tell a sinner endless reasons why he needed to come to the Savior. He could bring the unbelievers to the psychological edge of their own graves to imagine their own step across "the death line" into the after-life. He could mentally and emotionally bring the sinner before the bench of the Almighty for his personal judgment day. More importantly, he had gifts of the Holy Spirit working in his life that helped him realize the specific needs in a crowd. The Lord had already confirmed his preaching with amazing demonstrations of healing power.

An evangelist's work is to penetrate the crowd, to escort, figuratively speaking, each soul to a one-on-one, nose-to-nose confrontation with the Lord. Brother Bob's own conversion experience gave him the perfect credentials for the job because if his conversion was about anything, it was about being singled out by the Lord.

At thirty-two, the self-employed merchandizing artist was in Texas for a few days to visit a relative and shoot in a competitive rifle match, his beloved hobby. On a particular evening, his wife maneuvered him to a small Pentecostal church in a Hispanic neighborhood of Houston. An agnostic for some years, he hadn't gone to church much since he was a Catholic kid; and on this particular occasion, he would attend reluctantly. He had a splitting headache after being in the hot sun of a noisy rifle range all day, but at least he might get some relief in the quiet darkness of a church. As he stepped across the threshold he muttered, "I *would* like to know if God really exists."

The Lord must have seen his need for relief, except the church was anything but quiet and dark. During the service, a man stood up and made a speech in some sort of foreign-sounding tongue that Brother Bob couldn't understand. Then a second man stood and began to prophesy about "a stranger in the church from 1900 miles away." Brother Bob had never met the men. He had never met any of the people in this church. He didn't even know he would be going to this church until moments before it happened, yet the second man described this "stranger" as being at that moment in intense physical pain. The stranger possessed an unquenchable thirst for money and power, but he was spiritually bankrupt. The great exertions of his life, however he might claim they were for the betterment of his family, were pure selfishness. The visitor was a sham. He was a shell of a man.

Brother Bob understood this second speech perfectly. In fact, it was like he saw himself in a special mirror. The mirror didn't show him his outsides; it penetrated to his heart like a spiritual x-ray. The man's description of "the stranger's" pride and selfishness was so personal and so fitting, Brother Bob not only realized God existed; he understood that the Lord was cornering him. The cover was off. He felt naked while God in heaven was singling him out. This was no dark, cool church in which to quiet the throbbing in his head. Now his heart was throbbing, too, as the Lord put on the heat.

He didn't know what to do. His face flushed, his knees wobbled, and he just began to weep for his selfishness and pride. He felt destroyed by what God saw in him. No one in the church invited him to come forward, but on an impulse, he literally ran to the front of the church and dropped to his knees weeping. He might not know what to do, but he knew he didn't want to be the same man anymore. He would never think the same. He would never doubt God again. He wanted to change everything.

Even later, on the way out of the church, he couldn't stop crying. He couldn't stop on the way home, while he was getting ready for bed, or as he tried to fall asleep. He could not throw off his shame. His wife started to feel scared because it was her idea to bring her husband to that little church, but now her husband seemed to be having some sort of breakdown. That night in bed, while Brother Bob was preoccupied with his guilt, God singled him out again: "Go to church tomorrow. I have something for you."

When he heard the voice repeat the same words, he woke up his wife, "I think God is talking to me!"

Scared as she was, she knew better than to get in the way. "Okay, Bob, we'll go."

The next evening Brother Bob and his wife came to church expecting something important even though neither of them had any idea what it was. The meeting stretched long, but Brother Bob still hadn't received his promise, whatever it might be. He again moved to the front of the church and tried to make sure the Lord knew he was ready. "Whatever it is you have for me, Lord, I want it." The second the words were out of his mouth it was as though the Holy Spirit put his hand on Brother Bob's head.

The Holy Spirit felt like surges of electricity flowing into his head, through him, and out his hands and feet. For over two hours he was filled with the Holy Spirit. The surges penetrated Brother Bob's arthritic hip, the result of a hip dislocation he suffered as a teenager. At the time he never even thought of his old hip injury, but the Lord mercifully and sovereignly touched it with his healing power! He also didn't know why the Lord had picked him, but the Lord was transforming him inside and out. When it was over he could only think of one thing—getting back to Syracuse. He had to tell everyone.

Brother Bob's dramatic conversion in Houston seemed like credentials that would well-equip him for a life of evangelism. It was so obvious. He would just have to tell others what happened to him, and promise that the Lord would do the same for them. The Lord would single them out, too. They would feel shame, but only as the first step on a journey. The Lord would save them, heal them, fill them, and transform them! The Lord didn't love others any less than he loved him.

Back home in Syracuse, the Lord did indeed begin to use his dramatic story to turn many other hearts toward Christ. Brother Bob began to seek out any and every Pentecostal type of meeting. He found himself not only traveling all over New York, listening and learning, but also teaming up with a high-powered evangelistic team from out of state and sharing over and over again his dramatic conversion story, and praying again and again for people to be healed and filled. It only took a phone call and he would be there—church basement, restaurant, hotel banquet room, someone's kitchen. Driven by the urgency of God for saving souls, Brother Bob would tell everyone he met of the mercy and power of God. He would stop people in stores and parking lots to tell them about what Jesus had done for him. He would confront business clients in their offices. But the most direct route to saving the most people possible seemed for him to become a traveling evangelist.

The Lord had another plan.

In the early 1970's the Syracuse area was destitute of vibrant, spontaneous praise and worship. There was no church where the kind of radical conversions like Brother Bob's were welcomed or encouraged. As Brother Bob kept sharing his testimony and pointing people to the living Savior at homes and halls around Central New York, people began taking the same first step on their journey in Christ as he did, and a flock began to gather around him. Even so, he would only schedule meetings on nights when none of the local churches had services. He wasn't thinking of himself as a pastor.

He simply opened his home and let the people pray and worship freely. Scores of people would come. He used the Bible to challenge the people to change their ways. No matter how much the new believers didn't believe they could change, Brother Bob believed they could do anything with the Lord's mighty hand of help. The enthusiasm was flaming up as they sought the Lord for strength.

Before long, a need began to compete with Brother Bob's plan to be an evangelist. He could see it as plain as he could see the people pouring in the front door of his house for a revival meeting. The Lord wanted a new kind of spiritually empowered church in Syracuse. These people who had begun this journey with Christ now needed help along the way. Brother Bob could not help remembering how, in the Bible, Jesus felt compassion for an enthusiastic crowd that had begun to follow him, so he commanded his disciples to get them something to eat. Now Brother Bob began to feel a call to spiritually feed the sheep of the Lord. What about Bob Mazur, traveling evangelist?

In a way, Brother Bob was as alone as Jesus in the garden, a stone's throw away from even his dear wife. If he decided to become the traveling evangelist, who else would know that the Lord may have wanted something different for his life? He was sure, after all, that he could reach people as a traveling preacher. He could get results. He could work a crowd. Who could find fault with a successful evangelist?

But he also knew in his heart that "working a crowd" was not the Lord's will for his life. The Lord wanted him to do more than recite his conversion experience to others and pray over them. The Great Shepherd in heaven was calling him to become a shepherd of a flock of God down here on this earth.

As much as being an evangelist made sense to Brother Bob, becoming a pastor didn't. He didn't have experience or training. He didn't have the needed patience. He imagined he could continue working part time while he was a traveling evangelist. He didn't see how he would be able to support his family on the meager income of a pastor just starting a church. For every objection Brother Bob could think of, the Lord had the same response: "If I am calling you to do this job, don't you think I will give you everything you need?"

The resolution came when Brother Bob did as Jesus had done, not in a garden, but in his car in the parking lot of a local business. Day after day he would go to that parking lot and cry his eyes out to the Lord. At this crossroad of his life, where his own desire and the will of God parted ways, he told the Lord, "Not my will. Yours."

So Brother Bob began Living Word Church. As a pastor he did get to tell his conversion story many a time to win many souls to Christ in many an auditorium, conference room, and living room as he ministered the Gospel in Central New York. Thousands have come to Christ over these decades, experiencing dramatic turn-arounds like he did. Men, women, and children have been healed like he was, felt the power of God like he did, and taken up the challenge to change just like he did. The ministry has always, in a sense, been modeled after his own conversion, always been about the amazing ways the Lord can single out the hungry soul in the crowd.

In addition, the flock of God has required long-term care and guidance. Brother Bob found that he had to develop a fatherly kind relationship with the flock that he probably never would have known as a traveling evangelist. He has had to help Christian people marry, raise their families, be responsible citizens, and be servants of the kingdom of heaven. He has helped to make a spiritual home for many lost souls. Instead of bringing people to the edge of their grave imaginatively, he has literally helped many of them on their deathbeds as they faced the hour of their passing. Then he has comforted the survivors and taught them how to get ready to pass through their own great shadow of death. Today, almost forty years later, he is the senior pastor of a healthy, growing, giving church with all the trimmings of thriving local outreach, church school, foreign mission work, and more. We need not explain that such a success story can only come through a partnership of God and man.

The decision to be a pastor rather than an evangelist may have turned Brother Bob down the harder road—he may never know if it was the harder road or not—but many in Central New York and elsewhere are so thankful he answered the Lord as he did: "Not my will. Yours."

## CHAPTER THREE

# Until We Meet Again

*Genesis 4:8  And while they were in the field, Cain attacked his brother Abel and killed him.*

It probably takes less than ten minutes to read from the first verses of the Bible where God says, "Let there be light" to where Cain kills his good-hearted brother Abel. We wouldn't have even made page ten, and already our jaw muscles may be constricting. What kind of world did God make? What kind of start for the history of mankind is this—a brother killing his brother?

There is something especially horrific about Cain killing Abel because the world, at the time, was still so new. At that point in the record of humanity, the Bible has only mentioned four people as existing in the world—Adam, his wife Eve, and their first two sons Cain and Abel. Couldn't the first family live in peace? There is not even the consolation of believing that the murder was a one-in-a-million aberration. For a comparison, a little over three percent of the world's population was killed as a direct result of WWII. According to some estimates the Great Influenza Pandemic of 1918 killed about five percent of the world population. So by statistical comparison, Cain's murder of Abel was a monstrous turn for the worse. Was the Lord embarrassed?

Let's begin with a slightly more humble question instead: What can we learn about the Lord from the story of Cain murdering Abel?

Prior to the crime, the Lord confronted Cain: *"... if you do not do what is right, sin is crouching at your door; it desires to have you, but you must master it."** God saw the murder coming. Specifically, Cain's devotion to the Lord was sorely slipping, and the Lord was noticing. As the Lord knew, one thing would lead to another, and Cain would wind up hating his brother, if for no other reason than Abel was good. The Lord knows evil simply hates good.

Seeing the Lord knew Cain was going to lose any vestige of sense and good will, we may wish that the Lord had intervened to stop the murder. If so, we may have failed to see that the Lord did intervene in his way. We might find such intervention tepid, but he intervened by talking. He counseled Cain. *"Why are you angry? Why is your face downcast? If you do what is right, will you not be accepted? But if you do not do what is right, sin is crouching at your door; it desires to have you, but you must master it."*† Apparently, while the Lord was willing to speak up, he was unwilling to overpower Cain. He was not only unwilling to live Cain's life for him. He was also unwilling to stop Cain from living his own life.

According to the Lord's counsel, the Lord didn't have to master sin; Cain did. The Lord was helping in the matter by identifying the problem, but it was Cain who desperately needed to improve his relationship with the Lord, so he would not hate his brother. The matter would be decided by whether Cain would listen to the Lord. Ultimately, Cain had to master his sin, or his sin would master him.

As I mentioned, we may think that a brief counseling session, at a time when a man was building up hateful rage against his brother, was a weak response from the Lord. After all, the Bible calls the Lord "the Almighty." When a disaster occurs, it often seems natural to go hunting for someone on whom to pin the blame and to go looking first for the strongest

---

* Genesis 4:7.
† Genesis 4:6-7.

and wisest one at the scene. Bottom line: Management is always responsible. Who's in charge here?

The trouble is we cannot pin the responsibility on the Lord because, perhaps surprisingly, not even God can have it all.

To explore the idea that even God lives with limits, we can begin with the familiar riddle: Can God make a stone so heavy it is impossible for him to lift it? (Some people prefer a sillier version: Can God make a waffle so big he cannot eat it all?) Whether we say yes or no to the riddle, we seem to have discovered something it would be impossible for God to do. The Omnipotent may again be embarrassed. So what *is* the answer to the riddle? Easy! The answer is a resounding NO! God *cannot* make a stone so heavy he cannot lift it! —because it would be ridiculous for God to fight against himself. Additionally, in spite of the *no*, we will still think of the Lord as all-powerful. We accept the paradox: God is omnipotent with some conditions.

More to the point, God also cannot guarantee that a free world will be peaceful or loving. To guarantee peace and love would, like the "stone riddle," require him to somehow fight against himself. God could literally not guarantee that a truly free Cain would also love Abel. Love would have to be Cain's choice. Let me explain.

The Lord did not create us with a free will because he so delights in being democratic. He is not first and foremost a political revolutionary. Instead, he is pursuing an even greater good than our liberty. God is seeking love because, as the Bible says, *God is love.*[*] A difficulty arises because love can be built on no other foundation than freedom. Our freedom is therefore the unavoidable condition for his project of love. Not even God can change this fact. The Lord himself *has* to swallow, not a huge waffle, but the unavoidable condition of our freedom.

---

[*] 1 John 4:8.

42

Once he created us free to love, we were by necessity also free to hate. To repeat, freedom is non-negotiable in a project of love. The Lord will not abandon his purpose, not even to stop us from committing crimes like murder when he sees them on the horizon. To abandon his plan of love would require the Lord to fight against himself. He won't do it. He can't. God is love, remember, and he cannot deny himself. We can think of it like this: he will not commit a crime against us by overwhelming our wills. God will not become a thief by stealing our wills from us.

If the world is peaceful and loving, that is the doing of the Lord's free creatures as they work with him. If the world is fraught with trouble, the Lord's free creation is guilty of not working with him. We so often call the world, "the Lord's world," and so it is. He created it and does what he wants with it. He has, in fact, decided, in a large measure, to give it to us. In many ways, the world is our world, too, because we are as free as Cain was to work with the Lord or not. Will we make the world a sanctuary or reject the Lord's counsel and transform it into a house of horrors?

Actually, the freedom to choose is what makes us accountable. Freedom is the condition that gives sense to the Bible's reminders that the Lord will reward each individual human for his deeds. It's also the condition enabling the Lord to give crowns to his faithful servants. It makes sense to reward people for what they have done if they have acted out of free choice and are therefore responsible. It wouldn't make sense either to reward or punish puppets. The Lord will hold us accountable whether we want him to or not, but he will give us plenty of room to live our lives the way we want to.

Put yet another way, there is something more repulsive to the Lord than murder: *slavery.* The Bible describes God's creation of the first man. It says that the Creator breathed into the nostrils of a lifeless shape that he had formed in his gentle, skillful hands, and the shape became a living soul. It doesn't describe God attaching strings that make the shape respond to his every desire. He will generally not over-ride our freedom, even if the world becomes ugly as a result.

The Lord is willing, in his loving intentions, to exert himself with the greatest vigor to redeem this ugly world and then keep it on the track of righteousness. The Lord is not sickly or aloof. We see, for instance, the highest expression of his love and vitality in the person of Jesus. Of his own initiative the Father sent his Son down here to die for the ugly and save from sin anyone who will embrace him. In other words, the Lord loves and helps and saves at great cost to himself.

On the other hand, as high a price as he is willing to incur for saving an ugly world, the Lord has his limits. He is unwilling to do evil to do good. This is not an expression just to make your head spin! To be specific, the Lord hates tyranny, and he will not sin himself by playing the tyrant. He prefers a free world with disasters to a disaster-free world that he enslaves. The Lord doesn't even want to be the so-called "benevolent dictator." In fact, he refuses even to ride to power on our shoulders. In other words, he refuses to be a tyrant even if we want him to be. It's ironic sometimes how we get impatient with the Lord, or angry, when he is so respectful of us.

The Lord is good. Now he wants us to be. He will help us, but we must do our part. The Lord, as Ruler of all, insists that we do our part. In the first five or six pages of the Bible, in not only the Cain and Abel story, but in the Adam and Eve story, the Bible's writer established the most basic of principles. We're free. It can be unsettling to realize just how free we are, yet it's true.


I had a friend as good-hearted as Cain's brother Abel. Dale was as sincere, honest, and generous a man as I have ever met. A few years older than me, Dale befriended me when I was a teenager, and taught me a lot about how to pray. Early in our friendship we spent as much time teamed in prayer as we did doing anything together. As the years went by we did a lot of other things together, and by then I thought anyone could work with my brother in Christ.

Unfortunately there are still—we hardly need to be reminded—Cains in this world. To the entire community's horror, especially to our whole church's horror, and most especially to his dear family's horror, the man with whom Dale was trying to do business blew Dale away with a shotgun. Then he took his own life with the same gun. Dale is survived by his wife Linda and four children, twin girls and two sons.

It's one of those times when we are shaken because the Lord is not more willing to be a benevolent tyrant. The price of our freedom sometimes seems too much to bear. But bear it we must.

Did the Lord intervene for Dale like he did on behalf of Abel? None of us knows exactly what happened at the scene of the crime except that Dale was murdered by a man he faced, by a gun wound to the chest without any sign of a struggle. The killer was found dead nearby by a self-inflicted wound. But there is one more thing I do know. I know it because I knew Dale and some of the circumstances of that day. Dale, like the voice from heaven that reasoned with Cain, reasoned with the man who was about to kill him.

On an unseasonably warm, sunny Wednesday morning a couple of days before his death, Dale stopped by my house as he would from time to time when he knew I was home studying. We sat on the porch railing. On this particular day he was excited to tell me about a woodlot he had leased.

Dale was excited because he figured selling the quality lumber from the lot could make him some good money, thereby freeing up some of his time. No way was Dale just in it for the money. He wanted the free time for a very specific purpose.

Our church had recently decided to start constructing a large new building. To stretch our dollars the members of the church would do a lot of the work themselves. Dale, a self-employed building contractor, wanted to pursue his dream of volunteering full time for a year or two, whatever it would take, to finish the new building. That's what he came to tell me. Before long, he said, he would be on the construction site full-time.

His generosity took my breath away, but something about the business deal bothered me. Dale described how the man from whom he leased the lot was cranky and regretted that he had made the agreement. For several months the man would not even cash Dale's checks. Dale had been hand delivering cash payments.

I warned Dale to be careful. I told him that some people get so possessive about their land they will do crazy things. Dale assured me he could get along with the man.

That confidence was just like Dale. He was very courageous with people. He had a sort of faith in people as though everyone was family, as though anyone can be reasoned with. He was a gentle teacher, not a fist-pounding preacher. We know, on the day he was shot, he went out to the man's house to give him a cash payment. And, as I knew my dear friend, to reassure the man that the business deal would be good for them both. Then, as far as I am concerned, Cain killed Abel because Cain wouldn't listen to reason.

Dale's pleading with his killer would be like the voice of God to that man. But Dale could not and the Lord *would not* make the man's decisions for him. Instead, the man closed his ears to Dale like Cain did to God, and then he committed Cain's sin. We also know that the Lord himself was also speaking to Dale's murderer. In fact, his tormented conscience was greater than he could bear. After he saw what he had done to Dale, he tried to quiet God's voice with another shotgun blast aimed at himself.

Dale's murder is an example of a brother killing a brother. That's the way I believe the Lord saw it. And the truth is that the Lord had seen this horrible waste so many times before. All murder, even on the grandest scale—purges, terrorist bombings, genocides—goes back to Cain and Abel. How mankind has altered this world!

Harold S. Kushner, in the *NY Times* bestseller *Why Bad Things Happen to Good People* claims that we have to forgive God for making the world a sometimes very unfair place. We might think so for Dale and his wife Linda. But I disagree. God's only "crime" is that he is unwilling to steal or overwhelm our wills. His only crime is that he refuses to abandon his loving plan, which of a necessity, must really be founded on the freedom to choose. It's not that our freedom explains, by itself, all the trouble in the world, such as natural disaster; but all too often, we are the ones who need forgiveness, not God.

Every caring soul will want to know how Linda and the children have fared. They are well. Linda has amazed the church with her peace and resilience. She shines with God's glory as she cares for her children, bringing them to church four times a week, making sure they are in plenty of after-school activities, spending most of the summer frolicking at the church camp, taking them to the grandparents to learn crafts from grandma. The children are normal, fun-loving kids with lots of friends. Dale and Linda's youngest son is one of the best fishermen in the church.

Looking back, Linda mentions some of the things that helped her cope with the loss of her husband. She has shown us all, when tragedy falls, how there is strength in collaborating with God. There was the material, spiritual, and emotional support of her church family who surrounded her with special care. As the threads of life strained or wore thin, her brothers and sisters in Christ wouldn't let her out of the weave.

There was her God-given duty as a mother. She simply knew, whenever it was hard for her personally, that the Lord wanted her to be a good mom. At times it was the one thing she knew for sure. Linda would cry out to the Lord for her children's sake to be strong, and the God of the fatherless, as the Bible calls him, would answer her plea.

Helping Linda most of all was her faith that Dale is now in the place he longed to be more than any other, in the presence of the Lord. When Linda saw Dale's remains in the casket, she says it wasn't crushing because she knew it wasn't really him any more. She knew Dale was a praying man. But now he sees his Lord face to face.

Dale once wrote a song, probably the most widely sung of all the hundreds the church has sung in its decades of praise and worship. The song still invigorates the congregation every time we sing it, even though most people probably do not think of its writer. Linda, on the other hand, can take comfort that the words are truer for Dale now than when he was first inspired to write them.

I will love Thee, O, Lord, my Rock!
I will love Thee, O, Lord, my Strength!
I will call upon Thy name,
For Thou art worthy to be praised.

You bowed the heavens,
And you came down for me.
You bowed the heavens,
And the darkness was under your feet.
You came and lived the life
That would end at Calvary.
But God raised you from the dead,
And now I am free!

# PART II:  PROVIDENCE

## -- God's Intervention and God-given Opportunity

## CHAPTER FOUR

# The Thirteen

*Judges 6:38  Gideon rose early the next day; he squeezed the fleece and wrung out the dew—a bowlful of water.*

This bowlful of water was a true miracle.  Gideon left the fleece, a handful of sheep's wool, outside his tent.  Since he could tell it would be a dewless night, he asked the Lord to make the fleece wet even though everything else would be dry.  It was impossible, but it happened anyway.  That's what a miracle is—when something impossible happens, especially upon request!  Gideon meant the miracle to prove whether the Lord was really calling him to lead the army of Israel.

Being a hard sell, Gideon wanted to make sure what happened was not some sort of freaky coincidence.  A little sheepishly, he asked the Lord for a second miracle, sort of an improved variation of the first miracle, on a second night.  He asked the Lord that a dewy night would leave everything outside his tent soaking *except* for a dry fleece.  Again, it was impossible, and again, the Lord granted the result that proved he was in full support of Gideon.  The dry fleece was so wildly improbable it could not have been a coincidence.

Scores of sermons have been preached on how Gideon gained faith in the Lord even though he doubted himself.  He had to be convinced that the Lord was with him personally and would support him during his special challenge of leadership.  This is good preaching, but I want to point to another "faith"

Gideon did have, "faith" that the world works in some predictable ways when the Lord does not intervene.

Gideon's fleeces were actually God-experiments, conducted on two successive nights that should have resulted in a valid confirmation of God's will. Any well-designed experiment needs a control, in other words, a standard for comparison. The control in Gideon's experiments was his everyday life.

Gideon lived close to nature his entire life. He had already observed with perfect reliability that on a dewless night everything, including the sheep that had spent the night in the open air, would be dry. Running his fingers through the dense wool mat on the back of his sheep, he had never once found a soaking wet sheep after such nights. In contrast, on a night with heavy dew *everything* would be wet, really wet. In fact, the valley where Gideon was encamped was famous for "the dew of Hermon" that would descend from the high mountains north of the valley and enliven the greenery. After a dewy night, the sheep's woolly backs always carried a pound or two of extra water-weight.

Gideon's understanding of the way things work in the world was his other "faith." He believed the world worked fairly predictably. Gideon knew that his experiments on two successive nights were asking God to do something that he had never seen or heard of in all his life's experience. Because the fleeces were outside any natural explanation, they could only be understood as the intervention of the Lord.

The Bible is the book of God's interventions. Page after page tells of the great things that can happen when the Lord intervenes in the lives of his people. The truth is that we can hardly say we believe in the Lord, certainly we can't say we believe in the Lord of the Bible, if we don't believe that the Lord intervenes in amazing and improbable, even miraculous ways into his people's lives.

But if the world did not usually work in a pretty predictable way, how could we ever discern the interventions of an invisible God? We need the predictable and the natural against which to compare the Almighty's exceptional intervention. Gideon's fleeces were actually the exceptions that proved the rules. Rule one was that natural systems like weather systems control events in this world. Gideon got his exception to the "natural systems rule" with the impossibly wet fleece on the dry night. Rule two was a version of "Murphy's Law." That is, accidents and coincidences may be weird, but they definitely happen, mostly, it seems, when we want them least. Gideon worried the wet fleece was some sort of weird accident on the first night that was messing up his experiment. Maybe a sloppy soldier accidentally spilled a bowl of water exactly and only (and weirdly) on Gideon's fleece. The exception to the "accident rule" came on the second night. The fleece could not be accidentally dry. Two nights in a row proved the case indisputably. The Lord was with him! Hallelujah!

The point is that Gideon, his biographer, and the Lord himself demonstrate a fundamental belief that the world operates by a combination of natural systems and chance. In other words, nature's systems and the reality of chance are the standards. It's exactly what the Bible means when it says, *time and chance happen to them all.*[*] These natural systems and the laws of probability actually allow the intervention of the Lord to stand out in relief from a pretty consistent, reasonable, explainable background. In the Bible then, the exception, not the rule, reveals the special will of God.

We don't need the Bible to explain to us how the world normally operates. If simply living in this world were not enough to teach us, we could learn all we want about natural systems in science books and freakish accidents in *Ripley's Believe It or Not.* We can study the math of probability using rolls of the dice. But it's important, as we serve the Lord, to realize the Bible concedes that God is *not* directly controlling

---

[*] Ecclesiastes 9:11.

the normal operations of the world. The Bible's wonderful stories about the exceptional are its concessions to the normal.

Even when the Bible says of the Lord, *He makes grass grow for the cattle, and plants for man to cultivate,*[*] we are not to think that the Lord is directly ordering each blade of grass to photosynthesize. Rather we realize the psalm is giving God glory for putting into place beautiful and amazing natural systems.

So are the tragedies of life God's will? Life tells me never to say "never," but in the Bible, God doesn't afflict someone or some group without a prophet's clear warnings and explanations. In the absence of a reliable prophet, if we sincerely can't figure out what God is up to when tragedy takes place, he most likely is not up to anything. Whatever happened was a result of a combination of natural systems and chance.

How about when a child is born ill, retarded or even dead? Rest assured, it's not God's doing. It's an accident of nature. It's life. It just happens. There's no such thing as an accident?—people say that, but I don't believe it.

A fall from a ladder leaves a man paralyzed? It's an accident. We can explain what happened physiologically. The body can only take so much. It's a rule, that bodies break when they fall too far. The paralysis doesn't mean the man has sinned. It doesn't mean God wanted it to happen. It doesn't mean God is trying to coerce him or us into heaven.

A child is born disabled? Scientists are beginning to untangle the genetic and environmental factors that fell in place to create this terrible accident. For spiritual purposes, it's just life; tragic accidents happen in life. From heart disease to hurricanes—they are not trustworthy examples of the will of God.

Why did God make the world this way, where systems work, sometimes to the good and sometimes to the bad? Why do bad accidents happen? It's a long story. Let it suffice to say

---

[*] Psalm 104:14.

that it wasn't always this way. He put in place incredibly beneficial systems, but God purposely made a vulnerable cosmos. Through natural and spiritual deterioration, the systems tend to devolve toward chaos. The wear on the world is showing up, and right now, the world is a maintenance nightmare. Whatever its history, this fallen world is now our challenge. Like Gideon, we need to respect the laws, deal with the accidents, and ask the Lord for his marvelous intervention. We need to partner with God to improve the part of the world we can reach.

Like Gideon, after my freshman year in college, I felt the Lord calling me to help lead his people to a better life, not as a military leader like Gideon, but as a pastor. On one strange night the Lord confirmed his call to me. I wasn't seeking a sign like Gideon was, but the Lord did give me some confidence when he intervened on "the night of the thirteen."


On a whim I decided to drive out of Syracuse to visit a close friend in Rochester on a Friday night. According to my plan I wouldn't even tell him I was coming. My schedule required a late start, so I would arrive at my friend's house at about 11:00 PM. I knew neither my friend nor his parents would mind the hour because they were a fun-loving and flexible family.

While driving there on the NYS Thruway, I was praying. I was very relaxed and had no big ideas or heavy requests that I was praying about. I was just happy that I was about to surprise my friend, and I was praying that we would have a great weekend.

All of a sudden an impression hit me. It was the surest of impressions. I simply knew, more like *felt*, that I would share the Bible's message of salvation through Christ with thirteen people that night. It was a very specific impression. "Exactly thirteen people. Tonight." It never entered my mind that this was highly unlikely. I so believed the precision of the premonition that a mini-revival was going to happen that night, I began to laugh and sing songs of rejoicing to the Lord. In the day before cell phone conversations explained why someone seemed to be talking to himself, I am not sure what picture I presented to other drivers who passed me on the Thruway. Maybe it was good that it was dark.

After my private celebration, I began to think I should put on my "game-face." The Lord was giving me orders for the night. It was like an errand he wanted me to run for him, and even though I somehow knew it would happen, I also wondered if I would be up to the challenge.

When I arrived at my friend's house, he wasn't there. His parents let me in and gave me a sofa on which to crash, but they informed me that my friend, a year behind me in school, had his high school commencement earlier that evening. I should have realized it was graduation day, but I didn't. My friend's parents expected him to be out very late. I gave a moment's thought to that "feeling" I had received in the car on the way there. I didn't see how my mini-revival meeting was going to materialize, and it seemed to me, at that point, that I made this surprise visit on the worst possible weekend because my friend would be very pre-occupied with his fellow graduates. I fell asleep on his living room sofa, hoping to see my buddy in the morning.

Near one o'clock in the morning I thought I heard my friend come in the house with his characteristically bouncy steps. When he turned the light on in the living room where I was sacked out, that did it; I was awake. He was excited by the events of the day and also really surprised to see me, so his enthusiasm was electric. By then I was really awake!

After about twenty minutes of small talk someone knocked on the door. It was another one of the high school graduates. He was walking by at sometime after one in the morning and saw the light on, so he decided to stop. He also knew my friend's house had a very open-door policy.

I knew this visitor from our high school days together, but because I had already graduated and gone out of town to college, I hadn't seen him for a year. I began, mostly as a way to fill him in on the most important news of the bygone year, how I had committed my life to Jesus. I certainly was not trying to start a revival. As we talked the doorbell rang.

This time it was a couple. They saw the light while driving by, and were looking for something crazy to do on their graduation night, so they stopped. I was in the middle of my story about turning to Christ, so I just continued.

Teenagers can be brutally honest and pointed, and my friends were no different, so as I shared how I had committed my life to serving Jesus, they pried for my deepest motivations. They probed into a very sensitive subject: my mother had died when I was in ninth grade and my older brothers had already left the house. I was somewhat of a loner as a high school kid, and they wondered if turning to Jesus was my way of coping with grief over my mother and scattered family. To them, I had seemed, during high school, like a kid without a home. They asked me if believing in Jesus was filling some psychological need for me.

The probing took me off-guard. I had never answered this question for anyone before even though I had thought about it many times. While I wrestled to order my thoughts and find the right words, I felt exhilarated. A way to explain was coming to me. My turn to Jesus was bigger than the death of my mother or the loneliness I sometimes felt during my high school years, I told them. It was more like dealing with death itself. No, it was even bigger. It was dealing with *purpose*. Serving Jesus was about our purpose, life's purpose. Jesus had shown me my purpose for living. I told them that when my mother died, I was amazed how life just went on, how my father, my brothers, and the grandparents who outlived their daughter all returned to their jobs a day or two after we buried my mother's remains. But no one had talked about where my real mother went. Where was she? No one talked about what death meant. More importantly, no one explained *why we live*, I told my friends. But Jesus had embraced me and given me the reason to live. They listened, nodded, asked me to explain. I was exhilarated because I was doing it; I was sharing Christ! I was representing God to my friends!

Over the next couple of hours, two things happened. First, my old high school friends kept asking me more and more challenging and utterly honest questions about the Bible and faith and Jesus and life. I think they were overflowing with such questions partly because their high school graduation had fired them up to charge into a life that really mattered. Plus I had a very wholesome, God-conscious bunch of friends. We talked a lot about the spiritual hunger that God seems to put in us all, a hole that other people and things could never satisfy. People of all religions climb, scrape, crawl, build, sacrifice and pay to try and fill that hole, but the emptiness just seems bottomless. I was gladly telling my friends how Jesus had filled the emptiness in my heart.

Second, in spite of the lateness of the hour, more friends kept arriving by ones and small groups. By four in the morning, exactly thirteen young friends were around me, bleary-eyed but intense, sprawled on the furniture and cross-legged on the floor.

Thirteen people. That night.

A part of me wanted to run. I was a teenage kid. What did I think I was doing, trying to lead my peers in a discussion about the meaning of life? I felt so very humbled and unqualified. The other part of me was amazed to see Jesus bring the thirteen friends around me to hear God's message just as he had promised me he would. My friends helped me overcome my self-doubt, not only by testing me, but also by being hungry for more. Even though I didn't know a lot about the Bible myself, being a new Christian, I did my best to meet their interest with my enthusiasm. I kept telling them how, during our year apart, I had found out that the answer wasn't simply for us to try harder or be brave or smart. A life of purpose wasn't only about us and our experiments. We needed to work with the Lord. God sent his Son Jesus to us. God came in search of us. God sacrificed. God forged the way. Now we have to do our part, too. I read them passages out of the Bible, and we all shared our hearts with each other.

Through the night I was discovering that other people would likely respect the faith I had received from the Lord just like I had respected the faith of those who shared about Christ with me. People would naturally and spiritually be attracted to something I had that was truly good. I had received a gift from the Lord. I could succeed as a leader because other people would recognize heaven's imprint. As Jesus had said, *"Let your light shine before men, that they may see your good deeds and praise your Father in heaven."**

We ended the night praying together, two of my friends expressing to Christ on their knees that they wanted to be born again by his Spirit like I had been. Then we all went rejoicing to the local diner for breakfast, most of us with the conviction that none of this was an accident. God had intervened in our lives!

For me, hearing and responding to the call of God into a life of ministry could never be based on a single such story as "the night of the thirteen," however astonishing and exhilarating it may have been. Rather, the Lord's call would come to me in a multitude of special moments and challenges of faith over a period of many years. The first special visit of the Holy Spirit was when I was baptized at the age of seventeen and the Spirit coursed through me and literally gave me a vision of myself preaching. (Wow, did that picture ever come out of nowhere!) I sensed I would have to struggle against my preference for a more self-centered and reclusive life. I remember at the moment I emotionally and volitionally embraced the vision when I was still in the water tank, I

---

* Matthew 5:16.

literally trembled with apprehension. Somehow I knew I was to be stretched to near breaking.

There was also the challenge of informing my soccer teammates at Syracuse University that I was ending the athletic career I so loved, so I could better pursue the call of the Lord for my life. (They were so supportive!) Then there was my girlfriend. As much as I loved her, before we could even start discussing the possibility of marriage, she had to understand where I was headed. I wasn't planning on taking "the vow of poverty," but the provisions for a minister of the Gospel might be meager, I told her; the intrusions on our privacy might occasionally be incessant. We might ache with disappointment sometimes, when we would be misunderstood. (My future wife told me she wouldn't have it any other way!) My call was again tested when years of leanness came as predicted while serving the church, and my young family would eat beans and rice to help stretch our dollars and wonder how we could meet our financial commitments. (We never missed the payment of a single bill, and I can even say that I have recently begun to *like* beans again!) Another critical time occurred on my first visit to the Holyland, when on a lonely hill by the Sea of Galilee, the haunting melody of my guide's flute somehow brought into my spirit the voice of my heavenly Father's reproof. I had been too passive, the Lord told me. I was not to let anyone else set the pace for me. I was to lead. (I have since changed so as to never, hopefully, hear the Lord's reproof again!) At all of these special times I felt the risk of extending myself, the peril of freefall. It was the challenge of faith to release myself into the Lord's hands while I pursued a life of greater service.

I can't deny that a lot of confidence rose up in me as a result of "the night of the thirteen," but the rest of the summer was even more important. I continued to travel back and forth from Syracuse to my hometown specifically to share the Gospel with more of my old friends and their families. By the end of the summer many of them made commitments to Christ, many of them were filled with the Holy Spirit, and several of them decided to travel back to my church with me to get baptized. It was an important time for me personally because I understood by the end of the summer the same thing Gideon came to understand from his fleeces: I could be a leader of the Lord's people as long as I would partner with the Lord. My confidence grew as the summer progressed, but that amazing summer began on a night when the Lord intervened by collecting thirteen of my old friends to hear the good news of Jesus.

## CHAPTER FIVE

# Sweet Grapes

*Isaiah 5:4 "What more could have been done for my vineyard than I have done for it? When I looked for good grapes, why did it yield only bad?*

"What more could I do?"—who could blame a vinekeeper for being frustrated when the vineyard he cared for so diligently did not produce sweet grapes? We will read the details shortly, but he had done everything right. He put forth every effort and expense to be able to expect a good crop. But the vineyard produced only sour, even poisonous grapes. We might paraphrase his response: "What's going on here?"

The vinekeeper's questions are part of a larger poem the prophet Isaiah used to provoke his audience to do some heavy thinking about their relationship with the Lord:

*My loved one had a vineyard on a fertile hillside. He dug it up and cleared it of stones and planted it with the choicest vines. He built a watchtower in it and cut out a winepress as well. Then he looked for a crop of good grapes, but it yielded only bad fruit. Now you dwellers in Jerusalem and men of Judah, judge between me and my vineyard. What more could have been done for my vineyard than I have* *done for it? When I looked for good grapes, why did it yield only bad?*[*]

In my years as an English teacher I have found that poetry is not a pleasant subject of study for everyone. Some students are irritated that poems don't just come out and say what they mean. Maybe Isaiah had the same observation as I, because he explained his own song:

*The vineyard of the LORD Almighty is the house of Israel, and the men of Judah are the garden of his delight. And he looked for justice, but saw bloodshed; for righteousness, but heard cries of distress.*[†]

Isaiah laid open the symbolism: the vinekeeper was the Lord; the vineyard was his people. The wickedness of Israel and Judah had dashed the expectations of the Lord!

Rather than studying the sins of Israel and Judah, let's stay focused on the intriguing perspective of the Lord. The point for us is that God was disappointed. The disappointment is intriguing enough that some people may even wrestle with the idea. Let me explain.

A God who can be disappointed or irritated may seem too human to some theologians. They say that the frustration expressed in the Isaiah's poem must be some sort of a figure of speech. In this view, Isaiah's song is merely an imperfect poetic representation of divine thought. Unfortunately, this interpretation suggests that the entire Bible is an imperfect representation of the Lord and his thinking. The problem, say these theologians, is that the Lord's thought is actually so above our ability to comprehend that it must be brought down to our level, the level of the simple-minded (compared to God).

---

[*] Isaiah 5:1-4.
[†] Isaiah 5:7.

Such teachers liken Isaiah's song and other biblical depictions of God to the *goo's* and *gah's* that a mother coos to the baby in her arms. In other words, the Bible is not to be taken as real talk. If the Bible contained real talk about God, say these theologians, no one could understand it.

I can't disagree too strongly. To me, to interpret the Bible as only an "imperfect representation" or "baby talk" is a step toward hopelessness. It's practically surrender to meaninglessness. Doesn't the Bible have a more practical and comprehensible message than the nonsense syllables of a mother's cooing to her baby? Can we do no better than guess what the Bible might really mean?

Some theologians also decide (without even reading the Bible, really) that God is not God unless he is impossible to disappoint. These theologians connect all disappointment with humiliation, and they are offended with the idea that the Almighty may ever try something and not succeed. Their God, impossible to perturb, irritate, or disappoint, always gets his way and dictates every event, however miniscule, in the universe. This God certainly is glorious in power and knowledge. But is he more glorious than the God revealed in a plain reading of Isaiah's song, who is in some way vulnerable as well as resourceful? Besides, is it really imperative that we interpret the failure of God's vineyard as the failure of God? If God's creation were really as free and independent as the Bible often indicates, wouldn't that mean God is also innocent of mankind's sins?

The Lord who has created us with free choice also has, in his sovereign power as the ultimate designer, created a situation in which he can be disappointed. He has actually given himself such a harder task; he must be much wiser and more personable than the overpowering God of absolute control.

Let's risk an exploration of opposites. Is the Lord more like a chain-gang boss or a counselor? The boss of a chain-gang wears mirror sunglasses, so none of the prisoners can tell where he is watching. He carries a big gun and keeps snarling dogs that are the emblems of the power that keep his gang in line. In contrast, a counselor looks his client in the eye. He wisely persuades and educates his client so his client can better succeed after he leaves the counseling session. Doesn't the Lord genuinely teach as well as demand? On a scale from chain-gang boss to counselor, the Lord of the Bible often appears quite a bit closer to the counselor.

Must God, to be glorious, be so absolutely dictatorial over the affairs of humankind that it's impossible for him to ever change his mind? I hope we all agree that the God of the Bible is indeed glorious in his willingness to forgive us for our sin. We can never thank him enough for his willingness to forgive. So what is forgiveness if not changing one's thoughts and feelings about someone who has done wrong? The glorious God of the Bible, as an essential aspect of his character, is very willing to change his mind about those who have offended him.

When I describe God as moved by us, I do not mean to reduce God's power, and I don't think I am. The God of the Bible is awesome in power. But to be both powerful and responsive—that is glorious!

Is a God even alive who is so directly in control of everything that it's impossible for him to be genuinely disappointed? In a way, such a God is not free. He is himself a slave to a detailed eternal script. He can never improvise. He cannot change his mind. In fact, we wonder if he can think at all because all his thinking seems to have been completed in eternity past. He is actually straightjacketed by "being God." He has no active will because all his decisions were finished forever ago. He cannot possess courage for he is always in control and never in any way at risk. To me such a God is powerful but dead. He is too much like Aladdin's genie—a slave inside the confines of an eternal prison. Except there is not even an Aladdin to rub the lamp. It's not such a glorious picture of God. More importantly, it's not the God of the Bible.

A God who is so lofty that he is never really touched, in real time, by his creation, certainly does not inspire any sort of sympathy from us. His power inspires fear of him for ourselves, but never our concern for him. Yet the prophet Isaiah began his song of the vineyard like this: *I will sing for the one I love a song about his vineyard.*[*] "The one" Isaiah loved and sang for was the Lord. Isaiah's feeling for the Lord drew out of him a sympathetic song. That Isaiah felt sympathy for God did not bring God down or tarnish his glory. In fact, no man ever saw the Lord more *high and lifted up*[†] than the great prophet Isaiah. Isaiah both felt for the Lord *and* had the highest possible reverence for him. It's actually very biblical to care about the Lord.

In fact, we may recall the great detail the Bible gives, in both the Old and New Testaments, as it describes the sufferings of Christ. The Old Testament foretells his bruises, sorrows, persecutions, and even his pierced hands and feet. The New Testament describes him as the object of mocking, whipping, spitting, punches, abandonment, and finally death by crucifixion. We intellectually understand all this description is important as a theological proof of the price God paid on our behalf for our sins. But hard is the heart that does not also feel sorrow that God had to endure so much for us. In other words, hard is the heart that has no sympathy for God.

The idea of disappointing the Almighty and the appropriateness of having sympathy for him are challenging concepts. So to take a little break before our mental circuit breakers overload, I must tell you about a husband and wife at Living Word Church as representatives of *the vineyard of the Lord Almighty.* Only this time, the vineyard of the Lord produced the sweet grapes that God intended.

---

[*] Isaiah 5:1.
[†] Isaiah 6:1.

Dan's and Jenny's parents were already believers when Dan and Jenny were born. As children, they became so at home in the church, it would be common to see one or the other of them asleep on (or under!) the church's pews during some services that stretched a little long.

Church folks taught them Sunday school, babysat them in the church nurseries, and taught them from pre-kindergarten all the way through high school graduation from their church school. In time Dan and Jenny were both baptized, each when he or she had personally and freely committed to Christ and decided it was the Lord's time to get baptized, Dan at church and Jenny at the church summer camp.

But even more significantly than their immersions in the baptism tank at church or the pond at the church camp, the Lord used a variety of church programs to immerse them in his guidance, his presence, and his encouragement. The church also provided a strong formal education, athletics and theatrical programs, camping and leadership experiences, traveling opportunities, and more. The story of their childhood and adolescence reminds us of the Lord's treatment of his vineyard: fertile hill, choice vine, soil cultivated, stones removed, watchtower installed. Unlike the people Isaiah was complaining about in his song, Dan and Jenny flourished.

Dan and Jenny met and married in church. (It was my privilege to officiate!) Their circle of friends was and is mostly from the church. They have taken over their parents' trailers at the church's summer retreat. That's where you can find them most of the summer with their three young children enjoying the mutual support that the church's joyful fellowship creates.

Today, having become "sweet grapes" in the Lord's vineyard, Dan and Jenny have taken on some important responsibilities in the church. Jenny achieved her university degree in music education, especially so she could help the music ministry in the church. She often plays her violin in the church, teaches music appreciation classes and music lessons, arranges music for the church orchestra, and conducts the church music ministry. The arrangements she does for the thirty-piece orchestra are ennobling and energizing.

Dan received degrees in both chemistry and physics. He holds a position at a local scientific research corporation, but he has promised himself to reserve time in his schedule to give back to the program that helped him so much. He teaches high school chemistry at the church school and helps coach the varsity volleyball team. With his wife, he is an important part of the church's music ministry as a singer and instrumentalist.

These paragraphs are a meager beginning at describing Dan and Jenny's fruitfulness in Christ. The real fault of the description is that it probably cannot capture the becoming blend of happiness and seriousness in their attitudes. Theirs is a spirit that does not only come from church programs; their lives express their delight in living in partnership with the Lord.

The skeptic may be tempted to say, "Poor Dan and Jenny. Their entire life's experience is within the confines of one little church." In a way, the complaint expresses dissatisfaction for the wholesome and steady. Let's consider though: Do we really *prefer* people's lives to be the stuff of soap operas and TV talk shows? Has our TV and Internet culture conditioned us with a voyeuristic fascination with the ugly and kinky that makes us unhappy with their wholesome story?

Dan and Jenny would be the last to complain, and the first to retort. What's so "poor" about life-long friends? Is it even ordinary anymore to have family and church roots? Isn't the Lord a "family God"? What so bad about having a noble life-mission and a vibrant volunteerism? Teen pregnancy, rehab programs, police cruisers in the driveway, rap sheets, blood, bruises, and broken bones—who wants them? What's wrong with remaining a virgin until marriage?

Dan and Jenny did not become "soft" Christians because they were sheltered from the rough and ugly sin of the world by being sequestered within the monastic setting of a Christian school where mostly church friends surrounded them. Even as Christian kids, Dan and Jenny both had all the typical growing pains.

Jenny threw all the typical teenage tantrums over the grand issues of freedom and trust. She fought with her mom about everything from the suitability of the hemlines of her skirts to the plotlines of her reading material. Like two lawyers before the Supreme Court Jenny and her mother debated the sovereignty of the child over everything in her bedroom and that of the parent over everything under the roof. Jenny contracted all the same individuality-urges as any teen: for her own music, later hours, less chores, more time on the phone, car keys. Eyes rolled, feet stomped, doors slammed, crocodile tears flowed. One difference was that she and her parents kept praying their way through these stages, kept going to the Bible for guidance, and kept listening closely in church for the special message from God that would comfort or correct. For all Jenny's growing pains, the Lord was her compass, her anchor, and her captain. Another difference may have been that Jenny eventually found the size of her fuss didn't match the weight of the issues. In the end she embraced her parents' values as her own.

Around the end of high school a more weighty issue arose. Even though it lacked the unseemly and fleshy details, Jenny had an adolescent romance as emotionally straining as any in a teen novel—from the pre-teen obsession with the boy sitting on the other side of the cafeteria to playing the male and female leads in the school theatre production. Finally there was the devastation of the break-up when, just out of high school, Jenny felt drawn by life and God down a separate road from her boyfriend.

Jenny's experience as a Christian adolescent learning about love may have been easier for her because it was freer from the entanglements of sexual activity than the relationships of a lot of teens that are not so dedicated to Christ (That's not to say that Christian teens don't have all the same hormones flowing in their bodies as their unbelieving peers.) But it was in some ways emotionally harder, too, because she had to unravel an extra complication. She first believed that her boyfriend was God's choice for a husband. The realization that he wasn't came hard. It brought her to the verge of bitterness and cynicism. Jenny truly agonized until she concluded that she cared more about pleasing Jesus than she did about pleasing her high school sweetheart. It was the kind of decision that can test the mettle of a Christian at any age or maturity level.

And Dan. While he was making his decision to be a good grape in the vineyard of the Almighty, there were plenty of sour grapes nearby to ruin him, even in the controlled setting of a Christian school. Any Christian school has more counter-stories to tell than it can comfortably admit of "children of the church" falling away from Christ right under the watchful eyes of good parents, diligent pastors, and savvy teachers, right in a school that begins each school day with chapel and Bible study. Some bad apples surely tested Dan.

In about seventh grade, Dan hadn't yet learned that his class was entering the age of decision. Everyone would follow his heart sooner or later, the sour ones to rebellion. Others of his classmates would stumble their ways through the most awkward age of life with a renewed determination never to let Jesus down. Sooner or later each one's belief in his parents' wisdom in enrolling them into a Christian school would evolve. The deeper, more important decision would be about the Lord himself. Those who decided to serve the Lord are Dan's close friends to this day.

A look at one of Dan's classes, a small engine repair class, serves as an example of the spiritual struggle that goes on right inside the safe and Christ-centered environment of a Christian school. Brother Ernie, a frail ex-mechanic, living on his meager government disability checks, had volunteered to teach the class. Neither appreciating the personal difficulty with which Brother Ernie taught them nor the usefulness of the subject matter, the boys ran roughshod over their teacher with their punkiness. They resisted every chance to cooperate, and the sickly teacher was visibly shaken. It was one of those ugly demonstrations of the animal urge for supremacy that sometimes surfaces in middle school kids like the whitehead of a pimple. Brother Ernie diligently sent home notices of his disappointment with his class, Daniel included. As for Dan, he simply had not possessed the strength to stand against the real troublemakers in the class.

But the sting! When he began praying about the detentions and the bad reports, instead of just flowing along in what came naturally, a realization came to him. For Dan to work with the Lord, he would need to work with his teachers, maybe fragile Brother Ernie more than most.

The next school year, when (amazing as it may seem) Brother Ernie again volunteered, this time to teach an auto-mechanics class, Dan and some of his friends initiated a coup around the coupe. They didn't stage a rebellion against their teacher. They rebelled against the rebels in the auto-mechanics class. In so doing, they handed the class back to Brother Ernie. In addition, the teacher wouldn't have to worry about class discipline any more because Dan and his friends would take care of it "from the inside." At the end of the course Brother Ernie reported to all the boys' parents that the pleasure of teaching the reformed bunch of young men was all the pay he ever wanted.

Dan and the other boys didn't realize, at the time of their auto-mechanics class, how important their reform would become to them. The following year, their teacher couldn't teach the courses to a new crop of boys. His sickness worsened, and Brother Ernie finally died of his ailments. The student body elected to dedicate the entire year to him including a write-up in the school yearbook. Dan and his friends were relieved that they had decided to work on the Lord's side to help their teacher. Thankfully they had finished with Brother Ernie the right way. It was actually a relief to them that the stupid, rowdy behavior of an auto-mechanics class did not turn the school's yearbook into a mockery.

We can't say Dan's and Jenny's lives should serve as templates for every Christian young man or lady who grows up in the church. For instance, we do not pray that the Lord will keep every able Christian man and woman in the church of their births. We rather hope that the Lord will also send some gifted men and women to other needy places to help build the body of Christ.

On the other hand, what an example Dan and Jenny are of first getting the best of care that Christ, parents, and church can provide and then becoming productive! It's one of the most wonderful stories church leaders can tell. The Lord protected them from the emotional pains and scars that nobody wants or needs. He saved them from a mess of guilt and sickness. He kept them from embarrassing themselves. Even with all the Dan-and-Jenny stories already in the church I, as a pastor, would love even more.

We have to believe that one of the things God provides in his able care of his children is a set of parents. Perfect parents? Not likely! But the Lord can even use merely decent parents, in many cases, a single decent and determined parent.

In other words, a child going sour is not necessarily the parents' fault any more than it was God's fault when his vineyard went sour. We must know that even the best of parents may be disappointed by their child's decision to rebel against the Lord. Child rearing is not a science where rigid formulas always produce the same results. On the contrary, even the wisest parents and the most loving and nurturing home do not guarantee a child's decision to serve the Lord. This unpredictability does not excuse those parents who neglect or abuse their children. It does serve notice that decent parents shouldn't beat themselves up if their children take a wrong turn.

Likewise, different churches have a variety of intensity and scope in the programs for their child and adolescent members. The most important programs, in my opinion, are the strictly biblical ones of prayer, worship, vision building, and the study of God's Word. But even when big, wealthy churches and well-informed families also provide extra opportunities for entertainment, travel, culture, athletics, or even a full-blown formal education, there is no guarantee that the young will become productive Christian adults.

The human power to choose explains a lot. It's why two young people can grow up in the same nurturing Christian environment, and one can become a productive Christian adult and another, a troubling disappointment. Sometimes when rebellious children return to the Lord, church people will explain the rebellious period by saying, "All in God's time!" or, "They just had to learn the hard way!" Neither comment could be farther from the truth. God's desire was for those children to serve him all their days, not to take a sidetrack with the devil for a while. Those at-one-time-rebels could have chosen to be wise rather than bloodied and battered due to a period of rebellion. The Lord is never the author of rebellion.

God will give crowns and other rewards, the Bible says, to his faithful servants. It means that he shares with his servants the credit for the good that those servants do. In other words, God neither gets the blame when people rebel nor all the glory when they are obedient children of God. No more than parents should be over-praised if their children do well, nor overburdened with guilt if the children do poorly. The "grapes" of Isaiah's song, remember, are presented as an enigma. The mystery is explained by nothing other than the freedom of the human will to choose its destiny.

## CHAPTER SIX

# The Wayward Son

*Luke 15:32 "We had to celebrate and be glad, because this brother of yours was dead and is alive again; he was lost and is found."*

The celebration mentioned here was the happy ending of Jesus' story about the wilder of two sons who wised up and returned home. The young man fled from the home and disciplines of his boyhood and shamelessly blew his inheritance on a glut of partying, sex, and gambling. He came to his senses in a pigsty. A long dormant memory of his father's generosity sprouted inside him when the slop being fed to the pigs starting looking good to him. He thought: *"How many of my father's hired men have food to spare, and here I am starving to death! I will set out and go back to my father and say to him: 'Father, I have sinned against heaven and against you. I am no longer worthy to be called your son; make me like one of your hired men.'"*[*] Then he went home.

The foolish son had begun his death spiral with the words "give me": *"Father, give me my share of the estate."*[†] The request was the first step in his exercise of self-determination. His share of the family wealth would

---

[*] Luke 15:17-19.
[†] Luke 15:12.

73

provide him the independence needed to do great things, or so he thought. He wanted to make himself grand, follow a destiny of his own design. With little appreciation that his opportunity really originated with his father's legacy, he wanted to be a D.I.Y. guy.

Instead, he was caught in a whirlpool of waste and ruin. It's not so different than the stories today of big lottery winners or professional athletics stars who end in bankruptcy.

Was it foolish of the father to give his two young sons their shares of the estate? Hindsight suggests it was a mistake because one son wasted it. But if we consider the father's estate to be a gift of freedom and empowerment or a gift of opportunity, the father in Jesus' story is no more foolish than God.

God the Father has indeed bequeathed to all of us, wise and foolish alike, a gift of life. With life, God gives the capability to choose, making even the poorest or most handicapped of us, in at least some ways, free. With life we also have our love, compassion, and concern; our intelligence, talents, and creativity; our energy, strength, and ambition. They are all God's gift to us. Through the course of human history we have not always proven ourselves very wise investors of God's generosity to us, but that doesn't make God foolish, does it?

A father gives a plentiful share of a large family fortune to each of his sons. Common sense would tell the most naïve of fathers that complete loss is possible, and partial loss is probable. But he still bets the ranch. Why? He simply wants to see what his sons will do once empowered. It's more important to such a father that his sons try, learn, and care—in other words, *live*—than it is to preserve the wealth.

Remember that Jesus' story is meant to teach us about God. God, like the father in the story, wants to see what we will do with our lives. He takes pleasure in watching us even if it's sometimes painful. He sets us free to live, so he can watch what we will do. The Bible often refers to this trial under the gaze of God:

- Deuteronomy 8:2 *Remember how the LORD your God led you all the way in the desert these forty years, to humble you and to test you in order to know what was in your heart.*
- Judges 2:22 *"I will use them to test Israel and see whether they will keep the way of the LORD."*
- 2 Chronicles 32:31 *God left him to test him and to know everything that was in his heart.*

It's impossible to overstate how central this trial is to God's intentions for us. The test does not even have to come directly from God. Most often he merely needs to watch the way we meet the regular challenges of life. Put simply, life is a test to see if we will work with God.

The two sons in Jesus' story were being tried. The second, wise son illustrates what the foolish son could have been: responsible, respectable, and rich, in other words, an important man rather than the bedfellow of swine. At the conclusion of the story, the father reveals the key to the wiser son's success: *"You are always with me."*[*] Actually, success for both sons hinged on the one critical decision to work with their father. As strong, energetic, and innovative as the sons may have been, they needed their father's wisdom, self-control, and patience. A family makes a great team.

And if it's true that the only critical decision for his sons was to remain at home, the father was not just throwing away money after all. The wiser son was not really so wise. Both sons should have easily made the one simple decision to stay close and work with their father. Why not? The father, after all, had always been good to both his sons.

In the end, the wasteful son pulled out of his death spiral when he finally embraced humility. He replaced his

---

[*] Luke 15:31.

greedy words "give me" with the humbler "make me": *"Make me like one of your hired men."*[*] He had not only spent his family fortune. He had also spent all his pride and selfish ambition. His fierce drive for self-determination was gone.

In humility he accepted that redemption could not be a one-sided affair, but had to be the by-product of reconciliation. He became happy to put himself into the care, plans, and dictates of his father. In fact, that happiness-in-surrender was the greatest expression of his new humility. Maybe for the first time in his entire life, he was happy to work with his father rather than use him and run.

When a humbled son did return home, his father was watching for him, so as soon as the son turned the corner and came into view, dad ran to him. The father kissed his son, ordered his servants to clothe his son with a royal robe, put a fine ring on his finger, and kill a fattened calf for a celebration feast.

His pride truly broken, the son expected none of this. But even without the promise of a lavish reception, the son had come home with this assurance: at least his father loved him. He was ready to accept whatever his father had for him.

It's the same frame of mind that we need when we return to our heavenly Father from a life wasted on selfishness. In truth, the growth from *"give me my share"* to *"make me your servant"* represents the only path home to God. We need not worry about what we will lose when we come home to him. The Lord will not hurt us any more than the father in Jesus' story hurt his son. He loves us.


It reminds me of a young man in the church, David, who also has quite an intense father-son story. David had some personality traits in common with each of the sons in Jesus' story. Like the wise son he could be uncompromisingly

---

[*] Luke 15:19.

responsible. But like the son who ran off he seemed to live every moment like he had to prove his superiority. It made him egregiously competitive, argumentative, and combative.

Yearly challenged by David's inflated self-image, the principal of Living Word Academy, David's private church school, ratcheted up the pressure as David got older and ever feistier. Time-outs in kindergarten became detentions and suspensions in grade school. Ultimately, David insisted on his eminence one too many times, and the principal expelled him in eighth grade.

On the other hand, his combativeness could be an asset, too. Undaunted by his expulsion from school, a more careful David got himself re-admitted to the same school by sheer force of persistence. As the years clicked by, his quest for superiority also kept his teachers on their toes and made him a high academic achiever until he graduated high school. David's drive to prove himself then carried him to three stellar years in college in which he earned a four-year degree. Frequent debates with his professors and fellow students honed his analytical and rhetorical skill. So far, he vigorously defended the Christian beliefs he grew up with. Why was there always a feeling that something was about to explode?

Home and David's father were as important to David's success as the home and father were to the sons in Jesus' story. David's father Art has played the piano at Living Word Church almost since the church was born. Not much trained in reading music, his real gift is the ability to follow the Spirit's lead. Often, the preacher doesn't have to invite the sinful to the front of the church to pray. The melody from Art's piano draws them.

Having oversight of the church music ministry, Art has seen a lot of "egos" come and go from the church over many decades. Highly sensitive and self-important singers and musicians can require the wisdom of Solomon to keep them focused on the glory of God rather than their own. Art has been the needed shock absorber in the ministry, firmly attached to both the church as a collective effort and his co-workers as individuals. He has proven able to take a hit from two sides at once, and he was the same for his son David.

Art kept his arm around David, sometimes as an advocate and sometimes like they were in a wrestling ring. He advocated when his son worked his way back into Living Word Academy. They wrestled when Art, driven half by fright and half by wisdom, talked David into postponing his entry into a military academy. It's a credit to Art that he kept the strong arm on David as long as he did. Even David adored and respected him for it. Just the same, the inevitable explosion took place after David's third year of college. The fall-out was to continue for ten years.

David wanted to leave home for a full scholarship in Ottawa to pursue his master's degree. He had outstanding grades; he had gone toe-to-toe with his peers and professors in defense of his Christian worldview. He said he resented any suggestion that, if he left home to continue college, he would dive into the nearest gutter to wallow in the mire of immorality. He was out to prove he could stand alone. No family needed. No church needed. For the first time he squirmed so violently Art couldn't keep his grip.

Just as Art feared, school in Ottawa was the end of faith for David. A run to the wild side was probably what David really wanted for some time, and an intuitive sense of what really lay in David's heart was probably what drove Art to hold on as long as he did. The hold broken, David pretty much dove right into the nearest gutter of immorality.

Within only months the Bible became revolting to David. He retrained his rhetorical skills on the direction he came from, making himself as formidable an opponent of the faith as he had been the defender. By David's second semester, without a moral anchor, he became a frequent binge drinker, a carouser, and a remorseless womanizer. As he discovered new challenges in which to express his superiority, studies became uninteresting. When he lost his scholarship for his poor academic performance, he was forced home.

His return home seemed like a promising reconnection with home base for David at first, but he returned home frustrated, not humbled. Art still had no grip, and he confessed his prayer of panic to David: "I'm praying for you, son, that the Lord will bend your knee." David hated that. When Art would remind David of his on-going prayer during the next years, David would always tell his father to stop praying that. He hated to admit that the prayer scared him.

At home David was impossible to live with. He was trying to finish up course work for the master's degree, but he lacked his old discipline. Every paper was a day late. Often, his teachers wouldn't take his late work, and he would fail. He became depressed. He began hiding in video games. He fought and taunted and challenged his father, mother, and sisters at home. Art finally did what David's principal was forced to do back when David was a middleschooler; he expelled him from the house.

David didn't find peace on a study-abroad program in France even though he hoped to find it a "secular nation" whose liberal mores would make him comfortable. It turned out his hosts were among the three percent of the French population who were evangelical Christians.

He didn't find peace when he became interested in Julie, a woman he met on a weekend trip to Montreal. He liked her but made her miserable with his unceasing quest for superiority. He would be warm and generous until she began to get comfortable with him. Then he would turn cold to keep her off-guard. He invited her to France so they could live together; then he announced he didn't want a long-term relationship. He hated himself for giving Julie the Jekyll-and-Hyde treatment, but he just couldn't stop being David. In spite of the abuse, Julie stuck with David through his time in France and up until David enlisted in the US Army. He was about to marry Julie during his first leave after basic training.

When David had first tried to enlist in the Army, he was rejected due to a number of gimpy joints and the leftovers of medical procedures he had as a result of his rough and tumble life. True to form, he argued his way past the objections. He was determined to become a squad leader of a Special Forces unit. He wanted to face down a terrorist with a gun in his hands. He wanted to be shot at, earn a Purple heart or a Silver Star. He promised himself he wouldn't turn the shoulder from the oncoming bullet. But instead of shiny medals or a glorious death, David earned a lesson in forced humility.

Once during basic training he achieved a perfect score on a written test, so his NCO told him he could eat cake at mealtimes, a privilege usually forbidden to trainees. When the sergeant in charge of the mess hall challenged him in the cake line, David became indignant; the NCO who had permitted the cake was higher ranking than the challenger, he said. David hadn't yet learned the Army's obsession with compartmentalization. When it came to the mess hall, "sergeant on duty" was the master of the food lines, cake line included. The mess hall sergeant straightened up, stuck out his chest, and with a glint in his eye commanded David to dump his entire meal tray in the garbage—David was to miss the meal. In fact, the sergeant promised David he would be dumping his entire tray every time they met in the mess hall for the rest of basic training. During one stretch the sergeant ordered David to dump his tray seven meals in a row. He not only missed having a good meal for over forty-eight hours. He never tasted cake.

David once earned the traditional punishment for uppitiness, digging foxholes all the dark night, one rifle-length wide, two rifle-lengths long, and one rifle-length deep. Determined to show his drill instructors he was invulnerable to their mind games, he planned digging more foxholes in one night than they imagined possible. He scraped out four and a half with his short-handled pack shovel. In the morning, without a hint of admiration or surprise, the instructors simply ordered him to fill the holes and be quick about it. He collapsed several times. He was learning to be compliant when forced to. His pride remained intact.

At one point in his career, when a lieutenant recognized David's drive and realized he already had a master's degree and fluency in French, he recommended officer school. It would be the fast track to David's dream, the lieutenant promised. But to David it wasn't a dream come true unless he could climb his own way. If he didn't make his own way he wasn't superior, he thought. No, he told the lieutenant, he would climb through the ranks instead.

He climbed as high as sergeant. The old injuries that almost kept him out of the Army tortured him, but he knew better than to show it. He fought, he persisted, he cheated, he insulted. At one point he and another sergeant launched a private war with each other. David was so unmanageably competitive with this man that his commanding officer turned his back when the two sergeants literally fought it out in a pit. Thirty men stood above the pit cheering as if it was a dogfight. It seemed like David had finally found his niche in the bite-or-be-bitten life of the Army.

All through David's rise in both rank and rancor, there was Julie. David married Julie right after basic training and became a father while he was still in the Army. Julie had a difficult pregnancy, and suffered particularly because, being stationed with David in the service, she was away from her parents. Truth be told, she didn't get much support from her husband either because he was wrapped up with his army duties, even though, at one point, David locked horns with his commanding officer about his need to be with his wife through the end of her pregnancy. After more than a handful of complications, military and medical, Julie and David's first daughter was born prematurely in an emergency delivery. Thankfully the baby was healthy and thrived.

After his daughter's birth, David lost favor with his commander for not being sold out to his military commitments, and David figured he owed Julie a chance to settle down near her parents in Montreal. So at re-enlistment time, when David received an offer with US Immigration in Montreal, he left the Army. Salutes and rank had gotten old anyway. When his mom and dad visited David and Julie's new house in the suburbs of Montreal, Art reminded David, "I'm praying for you, son, that the Lord would bend your knee."

As he had for nearly ten years, David scolded his father, "Don't do that!" You would think he would have laughed. Real cynicism should have laughed.

But Art knew his son, and he also knew the Lord's blessing. The new house appeared like a blessing, but not unless the Lord was in it. As long as David was running from the Lord, Art feared that David's unending drive for superiority would inevitably drag the tender family into fights. It would only be a matter of time before David's pride would bring him to head-butting with his bosses, Julie's family, the child's teachers, Julie herself—who else was anyone's guess. The trail of lessons-learned-hard would stretch longer and longer. By this time, Art was not only concerned about his son. Julie and his fragile granddaughter wouldn't be able to endure the unending storm that seemed to swirl around David wherever he marked out a new territory to dominate. Then Julie became pregnant again.

When Julie was in her twenty-second week, David got an emergency phone call at work. Julie was at home bleeding. Her doctor had instructed her to get to the hospital quickly, so David rushed home to get her. An exam at the hospital proved Julie was dilating, but the bag of waters was still intact.

The hospital personnel were taking her condition casually because Julie had not reached the magic end of twenty-two weeks, when in Canada, a baby in the womb becomes a "human being." To the doctors, if the pregnancy continued five more days they might be locked in a fight for the baby's life, but if Julie delivered that day, they would consider the baby a disposable lump of tissue. A strange thought startled David: "If only we were home." He fought it off.

Julie continued dilating, and she started to panic. Could someone stop this? Was there anything someone could do? She didn't want to give birth to the under-developed baby, so she pressed David to do something: "David, pray for me and the baby, please."

"No, Julie, I can't. I just can't." Then he called home.

It confused David a little when his mother and father also became extremely concerned for the baby. They were on the way, they told him. They would call people in the church, so people could pray.

David didn't understand the tug of war he felt in his gut. He should be rational like the staff at the hospital and the laws of Canada. The thing inside his wife was not a person, yet. But his wife was panicking; his parents were driving five hours in a rush to be with them. A church was praying. An inconvenient memory confused him even more, of a classmate from high school who David knew had been born in the twentieth week of his mother's pregnancy. A classmate. A soul.

He was caught between the toughness and unbelief he had nurtured in his own soul and the faith and tenderness of the people who meant most to him. He found himself vulnerable to their faith. It was as though he could believe, too.

David vacillated between commanding the hospital staff to take action and thinking he was silly for doing so. He called the US Consulate and demanded that Julie be transported to a better hospital in an ambulance. Then, as Julie was loaded into the ambulance, he felt ashamed for making a fuss.

At the new hospital Julie became fully dilated and continued bleeding. Even so, there still were no regular labor pains. A doctor asked David for permission to induce labor and end the ordeal. Irritated at his own waffling, David steeled himself. He would not let this situation make a fool out of him, soften him, so he ordered a go-ahead. When the doctor pricked the bag of waters, and the fluid came out, it pricked David's heart, too. Remorse flowed into him. He told himself he shouldn't feel bad. It was the sensible thing to do, he told himself. Just the same, his jaw and eyes were slack with guilt.

At 11:30 PM a boy about ten inches long and weighing a little less than a pound was born. Julie insisted they name him Gabriel after the angel; the name means "Warrior of God." Gabriel was gasping because his lungs weren't fully developed. After patting the baby dry, a nurse wrapped the frail boy in a blanket and asked David if he wanted to hold his son. Gabriel's eyes clenched shut in pain as his little diaphragm heaved. The tiny warrior worked his hand free from the blanket and grabbed his daddy's finger. Julie looked over David's shoulder, and the baby quieted as he tired. She wanted to hold Gabriel, too. They took turns and sang to him for thirty minutes until he died.

David remembered all the times Art had held onto him. His dad was only trying to protect him, to save him from grief. Art had done his best even though David had been a squirmer himself, and David loved him for it. Even now his father and mother were driving hundreds of miles through the darkness to be with him. David felt he had failed Gabriel.

Always against the odds, David had fought to gain admittance to this school and that. He had argued with professors for his A's to prove his intellect. He clawed and scraped to get into the Army. He scratched and grasped to gain rank to prove his courage. Now he had given up on his son's life without a fight because of his stupid, fearful cynicism.

He suddenly wished he had done things differently. He didn't have to ask the doctor to induce labor. They could have waited to see if the emergency would pass. Weeks ago, he might have brought Julie to stay with his father and mother in the US where care for both Julie and Gabriel would have been more aggressive. As the little bundle grew stiff and cool

David remembered how Julie had asked him to pray, and he asked himself: "Couldn't I have at least asked the Lord to save my son?"

When David finished basic training in the Army, David's mother and father had seen David utterly drained of strength and energy. At the time, they thought he looked like he had been in a concentration camp. But they never saw him like they did when they arrived at David and Julie's house a couple hours after the baby died. David was drained of something else. His eyes were bloodshot and his face was swollen from exhaustion and weeping. David's shoulders were limp; his gait had no spring. His voice was barely audible, and he wouldn't pick up his chin. Art suggested they all try to get a little sleep.

No one should guess that Gabriel's death was God's *answer* to Art's prayer. God is not in the business of killing babies, so we will turn humbly to him as a result. First of all, such a thought contradicts the Spirit of God, who is love. God's Word, from cover to cover, expresses the highest integrity for God and the highest respect for each life. If God killed Gabriel to get to David, is he also killing all the other preemies who die, all the children in third world countries who die of disease and malnutrition, all the children who die by accident? God forbid! Gabriel died because of an accident of nature. Perhaps—we will never know for sure—something might have been done to save him.

The "something might have been done" is what made David wake up early the next morning with the same softness in his shoulders and voice. He might have done more. He didn't assume something could have been done to save his son's life, but that was beside the point.

Holding his dead son taught David something about himself. His hell-bound determination to protect his independence and pride had isolated him from God. It also made him embarrassingly weak and inept. He not only couldn't save his son. *He didn't even try.* The dead baby made him think he probably wasn't much sturdier, really, than that squirming bluish boy had been. He certainly wasn't superior. In truth he had not even begun to use wisely the gift of life that his heavenly Father had given him.

That morning, David bent his knee together with his father Art. David wanted to re-dedicate his life to Christ. He cried and prayed for forgiveness and to be purged of his self-importance. With his arm around Art, David came home in his heart. His soul had been dead and lost in cynicism and self-importance, but now he would live again.

# PART III: TRIAL

## --And God-given Power
## to Overcome

## CHAPTER SEVEN

# Prayer Warriors

*James 4:2 You do not have, because you do not ask God.*

In a way, this verse points an accusing finger at us. Things could be different if only we would pray.

Our first response to the criticism might be to point back at God. If God is God he has deep pockets, and he understands even better than we do what we need. Isn't it cruel of him to withhold help, especially when we are suffering down here?

God is holding out for a partnership with us. He seems willing to help us, but he insists on a relationship with us first, so that our asking becomes the key that unlocks the help. The act of asking begins our relationship with the Lord and then keeps it vibrant. In fact, the imperative of prayer is this strong: even Jesus, God's Son, needed constantly to pray to his heavenly Father.

God is not being coy or self-important by requiring us to ask before he intervenes in our lives. He created us to be in a relationship with him. Sharing life with him, including talking to him, is our very purpose. Like the expertly fitted component of a master's craft, praying keeps us fastened. If we truly enter into a relationship with him, starting with asking him for help, we will be the ones to benefit the most.

It's not as though there is little to pray about. If we start with our personal needs, the list can quickly fill a prayer journal. If we begin to consider the needs of our communities, nations, and world, the list becomes beyond imagining. We need more peace between nations, factions, families, and individuals. The poor, the sick, the elderly, the children, and other disadvantaged people need more concern and help from those who can give it. We need healings of our thoughts, our feelings, our bodies, and our earth. The world needs relief from hunger, filth, and violence. We need repentance from pride, self-centeredness, anger, and doubt.

Maybe only God seems big enough to blame meaningfully for this bottomless pit of need, but is the neediness of this world really God's doing? Is the world needy simply because God has willed it so? This line of thinking robs us of resolution in prayer. If we think the spiritual and material poverty in the world is God's will, it's going to be hard even to talk to him without feeling like we are fighting him. Or we may be intimidated by the enormity of the task before us, so that we lack even the gumption to make a little start.

When it comes to getting a small start on an enormous task, I like the example of a pastor friend in India, Brother Charles. He is faced with incredibly widespread need every day in a religiously and economically poor nation. He has very meager material resources with which to make a difference. Where can he start? Blame God? Instead he once bought a single watermelon! An extremely impoverished ethnic group in India called Yanadi lives along a waterfront. The Yanadi children had probably never eaten a watermelon. So Charles bought a watermelon, cut it into inviting slices, and left it on a table where the Yanadi children could get it. Then Charles moved away to a balcony where he and the children could see each other from a distance. A little gang of children slowly approached the watermelon, wondering if Charles would throw something at them or call the police. He just watched quietly as the children finally sampled the treat. Before long they were driving sugary pink pulp into their mouths right up to the rind. The juice ran down their chins as they glanced about furtively.

Charles' smile told them there was no worry; the watermelon was a gift. So began a church and a children's home for some of the poorest of the poor in India. Likewise in prayer, we just have to start. We can petition the Lord for one simple victory. Then we can make adjustments to what we are praying about as we proceed.

Some people will not even start praying because they don't see how praying will help anything. On the contrary, James said, *You do not have, because you do not ask God.* It's not that this little sentence captures the one all-encompassing explanation for the neediness of our world. But it does help in this sense: it tells us of an answer we may be neglecting.

When he penned his words James was following the lead of Jesus Christ who said, *"If you, then, though you are evil, know how to give good gifts to your children, how much more will your Father in heaven give good gifts to those who ask him!"*[*] Jesus always encouraged us to have faith in the Father's care but never a passive faith. Rather than teach us to be martyrs to all that ails us, he always encouraged us to have an active relationship with the Father and him. An animated relationship begins with talk. Jesus said, *"Ask and it will be given to you."*[†]

When we see trouble and neediness in this world, we should not, as I pray this book is showing, assign God as the first cause, as if God wants us to suffer or he is punishing us or coercing us. Neither can we automatically blame ourselves even though we should honestly measure our contribution to our world's trouble. However, we *should* take squarely on our shoulders the first responsibility for finding relief. One way to bring relief is through prayer, and the Lord is waiting to hear from us.

Several possibilities are worth considering to increase the productivity of our prayer: asking the Lord more, of course;

---

[*] Matthew 7:11.
[†] Matthew 7:7.

asking the Lord with the right attitude; asking with all our hearts; praying with faith; even though some people are asking the Lord, more of us needing to; coming to the Father in the name of the Son. Jesus did say, *"I will do whatever you ask in my name, so that the Son may bring glory to the Father. You may ask me for anything in my name, and I will do it."*[*] There is a good chance that many of us, even those of us who are suffering or have loved ones suffering, haven't asked the Lord for his help at all. Others may have quit.

Even though compassion compels us to grant that there is no prayer as sincere as that of the suffering soul, a number of attitudes render even some of their prayer as suspect. Suffering souls sometimes toss up a prayer in the "hey, you never know" spirit of the state lottery. People don't think they have much to lose in "saying a prayer" or lighting a candle, so they do it. Should we expect God to take such "prayer" as earnest?

Sometimes the request, "Pray for me," is really a request for pity. We can be glad that those who are suffering feel willing to ask for pity, but the request for pity, even if it's worded, "Pray for me," is not really prayer to God. This analysis is not meant to kick someone when he is already down, but it does indicate we need to look a little more deeply for real prayer.

Some people approach praying as a rite, like an incantation or magic formula. They do so when they repeat stock prayers that have little connection to what is going on in their hearts or the hearts of those who are suffering. Such a prayer, if it can be considered prayer at all, is not about having a relationship with the Lord. Truly, it's an attempt to manipulate the natural world by overriding it with supernatural control systems. In other words, it's sorcery. Truthfully, a lot of ritualistic "prayer" in many churches falls under this description. Jesus, the great teacher of prayer, actually warns us against substituting thoughtless ritual for prayer: *"When you*

---

[*] John 14:13-14.

*pray, do not keep on babbling like pagans, for they think they will be heard because of their many words.*[*] The "Lord's Prayer," though based on the teaching of Jesus, is sometimes used in paganistic repetitions.

I have often seen suffering people settle within themselves that it's God's will for them to suffer, so they ask only for strength to endure. The request for bravery and fortitude is a safe and good prayer, but is that all we can ask for? The Bible seems to say we could have more significant answers if we would only ask specifically for them.

The prayer James and Jesus spoke about is the honest, humble talk of children to their loving Father. The world isn't the way the Lord intended it to be. He is waiting to hear from us about what we see and feel. Do we realize that we can make a difference by collaborating with the Lord in prayer? The Bible encourages us to pray with innumerable marvelous accounts of answered prayer. Right now we need a story of answered prayer that is close to home.


One day at home Karen, a mother of three young children, was having the same pains in her chest and numbness in her neck that had been dismissed by several doctors as "anxiety attacks." Her husband Gene, a family doctor, decided to hurry her to the emergency room while the symptoms were still present to confirm positively that nothing was physically wrong. Then things began to happen incredibly fast.

The ER doc asked Gene to come aside and view a chest x-ray. Gene saw the ominous shadow for himself—a mass centered under the chest bone! He looked at the name printed at the bottom of the film, sure it could not be his wife's, but a shudder began at the back of his neck and traveled to his knees. This wasn't just an instructional exercise. There was Karen's name.

---

[*] Matthew 6:7.

The "C-word" floated like a bubble in and out of the fog in Gene's mind. He hadn't expected to come to the hospital and be the one having an anxiety attack, but the wind was knocked out of him. Gene returned to the exam room weeping. There was no way to ease into this.

He and Karen talked, considered the worst, held each other, and cried, not sure if the embrace was the beginning of a painful good-bye. As a doctor, Gene's mind was already swirling with detailed nightmares. Karen was simply in shock.

Within the next days, tests confirmed the worst. A large non-Hodgkin's lymphoma tumor was invading Karen's chest cavity, compressing the superior vena cava, and choking off the circulation of blood between her lungs and head. She was facing what could be the last fight of her life, but no one was blaming God for her illness. It was time to go into "prayer mode."

Our church has four regular services every week. From the time of her diagnosis, Karen and Gene were there every meeting possible, and the target of every session of prayer and worship for them was Karen's cancer. Sometimes Karen had to fight through exhaustion and discomfort to make it to church. Sometimes Gene had to go alone. Karen needed her health; Gene needed his wife; the children, ages 8, 6, and 4, needed their mother.

Every time Gene could attend a church meeting he would spend worship time at the rail at the front of the church. He prayed so loudly and incessantly and specifically for his wife anyone in the church could make out his petitions to God. "Lord, heal my wife!" No one minded. The entire church often put their own needs aside while they joined Karen, Gene, and the children in prayer. There was no holding back. It was actually a little scary to try so hard in prayer because we all knew the harder we tried, the greater could be the pain of disappointment. So it went for six months.

Gene was drawn to making a quick study on every treatment and prognosis related to Karen's cancer, so he could take control of her treatment. It would feel better to fight than trust the specialists and wait. But the Lord calmed him down and gave him better sense. As closely as he would follow his wife's case, he would leave the medical protocols to the specialists.

Instead the doctor began to study prayer in the Bible. He studied who should pray, when to pray, where to pray, and what to pray. He studied faith. He did not get promises from the Lord that his wife would recover. Instead he received strength, even good cheer from studying the Word of God. The message he heard the most was, "Work at prayer."

Prayer was not, of course, the lone strategy. Karen and Gene did indeed consult specialists. Chemotherapy was designed and implemented, six rounds, one every three weeks. Regular tests were performed. But to the horror of all, the tumor shook off everything the docs threw at it. It was growing, and the symptoms were getting worse. The health insurance company was starting to balk at proposals for expensive new treatments because Karen's life was looking to them more and more like a done deal.

Karen and Gene accepted the recommendation of local doctors to bring Karen to the Dana Farber Cancer Institute in Boston, MA for the most radical treatment possible. Once there she would receive a powerful radiation therapy at the same time as a bone marrow transplant. The aggressive attempt to save her could kill her. All the while, the fight of prayer continued. Then came the climax.

Karen lay quarantined in a hospital bed in Boston, few visitors allowed, none unless scrubbed, gowned, and masked because the bone marrow transplant left her immune system severely weakened. She was exhausted. She couldn't even drink a sip of water. Her chest and back were burned boiled-lobster red from radiation therapy. Adhesive tape would not hold her bandages in place over her medicine port because the glue on the tape would simply peel away her blistered flesh. One day toward the end, Gene looked down at his bloated, bald wife, and clamped his jaw. A doctor had just given him a bleak prognosis.

Unless Karen could start producing more white blood cells within the next few hours, a deadly fungus would likely infect her blood. Worse, the only medicine for combating the infection, amphotericin, usually fails with bone marrow recipients. Worse yet again, amphotericin creates a torturous ordeal before the patient succumbs. Ampho-*terrible*, Gene thought. Karen was almost asleep. He wouldn't tell her. Sometimes all the months of talking seemed like a waste, and now he was exhausted to the marrow, too. The husband-doctor was finally ready to accept his role as life's punching bag.

"I'll see you in the morning, honey." He gently patted his wife's forehead and went home.

Gene still didn't want to talk, not even to God, six hours later when he rolled out of bed. On this morning, prayer started as a mere routine he had learned during months of fighting against Karen's cancer. He shoved aside some shirts and slacks, and ducked into the closet. His nose against the floorboards, he felt detached from himself, a strange man in a closet mumbling to heaven but rehearsing in his mind, just as he had all night, the miserable prognosis from the previous day. But a meager flame ignited in Gene's spirit.

Spirit and speech joined for one last, desperate go: "Lord, I can't take it any more. Karen, Lord—heal my wife! Please, O Jesus! Please, O Jesus! *Please, O Jesus!*" He silently listened like he had just fired a mortar round and was expecting to hear a blast from the other side of the hill where he had aimed.

Then a thought flashed: "When I healed the ten lepers, only one came back with thankfulness. Give God glory like he did." The flash hadn't come from Gene. Give glory to God like a leper Jesus *healed*? Gene straightened upright on his knees and sat back on his heals.

At the same time, Karen was awake, too. It had been a nearly sleepless night because nurses kept intruding, monitoring her temperature, changing her bandages, and taking blood. Just the same she felt like getting up. She went to the sink to do her special mouth care. A drink of water was refreshing and tasted good for the first time in weeks. Weird. A funny thought came to her of how, in the Bible, a man thought of himself as a beast—*I was a brute beast before you*—but the Lord still loved him—*You have taken hold of my right hand.*\* Karen was sure she was like that man. She looked out the window and wondered what kind of day it would be...looked good. That was weird, too—caring about the weather. What had happened in the night?

Gene made it to the hospital before long. When he rounded the corner to step into Karen's room, he stared. The room was bright. Karen was sitting up in bed. The rims around her eyes were not red and raw any more. She looked more rested than she had looked for weeks. Chin down, Karen pointed, "Look, Gene!"

Her chest, the skin that only some hours before was so raw the tape wouldn't hold, was forming islands of soft, white skin. A clean gauze pad was *taped* over her medicine port. A nurse, no surgical mask covering her beaming smile, came in and gave Gene the report. Karen's temperature was normal. Her white blood count was up. "The doctor will probably send her home in a day or two."

Gene had never witnessed such a dramatic transformation in his medical career. He had never heard of anything like it in a medical text. The only place he had read of something like it was in the Bible—Jesus had healed the ten lepers.

It can be disconcerting sometimes when a devastating illness strikes how "the world just keeps spinning." The kids still have to go to school, the bills still have to be paid, the job needs tending, and all the other people we are connected to go forward in their routines. Life can be cold.

---

\* Psalm 73:22-23.

The same can be said sometimes of a miracle. Someone should organize a parade. Light the fireworks. Call the band. Order a cake. Instead, Karen was healed a few days before a new school year started. The immediate challenge was so mundane: get the children back to Syracuse in time for the first day of school, but then rush back to Boston to check Karen out of the hospital and bring her home! As disconnected as the details seemed, how wonderful it felt to have to manage the mundane!

They managed. And since then, over seven years now past, both Karen and Gene have determined not to let the mundane affairs of life cool their thankfulness toward the Lord's hand, which so graciously touched Karen. They have determined to be like the one leper out of ten that Jesus healed who "gave God glory." They are still so thankful to share their story.

I am obviously thankful to tell their story, as well, even though I understand that there may be a cruel side in the telling. Some people may be raw because of someone who has prayed but *not* received. A prayer warrior may be offended with the idea that someone prayed harder or better, so they received God's favor.

We are not trying to say we can control our futures if we will only pray harder. Many of us know that we *have* prayed. We prayed hard. We prayed with faith. We enlisted the help of our friends and congregations in prayer. Yet a loved one did not get healed. I have myself prayed for many suffering people who, after dedicated prayer, had to carry on without physical relief from their terrible ailments. We won't say they did not receive strength to carry on and peace at the approach of death, but many continued suffering physically. Many of them have died.

But I have concluded that it's not at all cruel to tell Karen and Gene's wonderful story of answered prayer. It's not the only story of God's healing touch that I have witnessed.

It's not necessarily the most dramatic story. Let's not, however, compare miracles.

In addition, I do think it would be wrong to look at Karen's amazing blessing with ugly envy. I mean, we should not allow the existence in any dark corner of our hearts a malicious wish that Karen was not healed. Only the devil's envy says, "If I can't be healed, I don't want anyone to be healed."

Rather, I pray that Karen and Gene's ordeal will encourage us, even challenge us all, to work hard at prayer. May we accept our God-given responsibility to search in prayer for relief to suffering in our families, neighborhoods, among our friends and co-workers, and beyond. May we never fault someone who asks the Lord for the best. Prayer changes things.

## CHAPTER EIGHT

# "Jesus-Man"

*Job 1:9-10 "Does Job fear God for nothing?"*
*Satan replied. "Have you not put a hedge around*
*him and his household and everything he has?"*

Satan's name in Hebrew means literally "The Adversary," and here we see him doing his adversarial thing by accusing the Lord. This time the Adversary was right about at least this much: God had indeed put a protecting hedge around his servant, a man named Job.

Prior to Satan's accusation, the Lord had asked him, *"Have you considered my servant Job? There is no one on earth like him; he is blameless and upright, a man who fears God and shuns evil."** But Satan's mind was stuck on the hedge of protection rather than Job's alleged piety.

To be precise, the Adversary objected to the Lord's method of assessing Job. He claimed that the Lord's protecting hedge around Job was creating an unfair situation. The criticism was sinister. Job was being coerced by a Godfather who offered protection for obedience. Job's godliness was actually being bought with prosperity. We could translate Satan's accusation in verse nine from the Hebrew original, *"Does Job fear God freely?"*

---

* Job 1:8.

Even though Satan's notoriety as a liar certainly preceded him, his objection must have had some merit because the Lord agreed for Satan to strip Job of wealth, children, and health. Then Job's character could be reassessed without any tinge of favoritism.

Put in the terms we have been using in this book, Satan accused the Lord of *not* requiring Job to serve the Lord in a world that was operating freely. The Lord was stacking the deck for Job by removing any chances for accidents and disasters from his life. Satan's objection restated: "Why are you allowing him to be the exception?"

The Lord conceded to Satan's gambit by letting go of the controls in Job's life. In other words, the Lord would not continue tampering with the rough and ugly free world, not even for a favored servant, not even if the criticism came from a desperate and despicable enemy.

Satan lost no time in retaliating for the Lord's coddling of Job. Even though Satan had successfully taken the moral high road by accusing God of manipulating the world in Job's favor, he was not then about to play fair himself. The Lord's enemy began pushing every button and pulling every lever to press out of Job a single sinful confession. The Adversary would not be satisfied in this experiment if Job's suffering were merely "average." He intended to stretch Job on the tormentor's rack.

Thieves stole much of Job's livestock and murdered many of his servants. Fire destroyed the rest. A great wind collapsed a house upon his children, killing them all. Then when Satan accused God of still protecting Job, God gave Satan even more room in which to ply his torture trade. The Adversary afflicted Job's own flesh with a pox. Job sat on an ash heap scraping his open sores with pieces of broken pottery, his grieving wife complaining in his ear.

What does Job's suffering mean to us? I do not believe the lesson is that all of the world's crime, sickness, and natural disaster are the handiwork of Satan. In fact, such a lesson ignores God's concession to Satan's evil plan, a concession that looms over the details of Job's suffering. We need to work our way to a better explanation of this extraordinary confrontation of God and Satan.

In the large middle section of his story, Job complained in a series of deep and poetic theological meditations. Basically, Job wondered how the Almighty God could so coldly and unjustly afflict an innocent man as himself. Job's exasperation bordered on indignation and impudence: *"If only I knew where to find him; if only I could go to his dwelling! I would state my case before him and fill my mouth with arguments."*[*] Job was positive that life should make more sense than his did, and he wanted to hold God accountable for the chaos. He wanted to bring a malpractice suit against God! In fact, from the readers' perspective, the book of Job hardly hides the concession of God to the dastardly plan of the Adversary. If we were on the jury with Job as plaintiff, our sympathies would probably lie with Job.

Alternating with Job's complaints were the discourses of three "friends" who felt compelled to take God's side in the face of Job's ranting. They insisted Job's suffering had to make sense because everything that goes on in this world expresses the purposes of the Almighty. They insisted that, in his absolute control of the world, God blesses the good people and brings trouble on the wicked. So Job only needed to be honest, they argued. The only logical conclusion of their faith in God was that Job needed to admit the truth—Job must have sinned. Job's suffering must have been God's justified pressure on him to humble him before the Almighty. Again from the readers' perspective, our sympathies are with Job. What unjustified emotional suffering Job's friends heaped on him when he was already in excruciating pain! As the old saying goes, "With friends like these…!"

---

[*] Job 23:3-4.

Outnumbered three to one, Job impressively held his ground, achieving what appeared to be a stalemate (I am simplifying by leaving out the discourses of Elihu). Then the Lord dramatically interrupted with a surprising and ironic double pronouncement.

To his friends: *"You have not spoken of me what is right."** To Job: *"Who is this that darkens my counsel with words without knowledge? Brace yourself like a man; I will question you, and you shall answer me."†* And here comes the true point of the book of Job. Neither Job nor his friends understood how a truly free creation must of necessity be susceptible to trouble. All the claims of both sides were based on an erroneous assumption that God manages (or should manage better) all the affairs of this world. In short, all four of them, Job and his three "friends," were wrong.

In the Lord's majestic explanation to Job, he referred at length to a sea monster called the leviathan, who many scholars believe symbolizes evil as a force in the world, perhaps even Satan, who is known elsewhere in the Bible as *that old serpent.* Out of a whirlwind, the Lord questioned Job,

> *Can you pull in the leviathan with a fishhook or tie down his tongue with a rope?*
> *Can you put a cord through his nose or pierce his jaw with a hook?*
> *Will he keep begging you for mercy? Will he speak to you with gentle words?*
> *Will he make an agreement with you for you to take him as your slave for life?*
> *Can you make a pet of him like a bird or put him on a leash for your girls?‡*

---

* Job 42:7.
† Job 38:2-3.
‡ Job 41:1-5

Of course, no mere human could control the leviathan! More to the point, although the Almighty can control the monster, not even he tames it. The Lord said of the beast, *"Any hope of subduing him is false,"*[*] and *"He is king over all that are proud."*[†] The poem therefore describes an ongoing battle of wills, the unruly will of the leviathan pitted against a master's desire for order and peace.

The Lord prefers battling with the beast to destroying it. The Lord's position is like that of the policeman—a cop can't shoot every suspect who calls him names and criticizes his work simply because he is involved in a battle of wills. Likewise the Lord, being that he is *both* good *and* committed to a free world, has his mighty hands full when it comes to controlling evil. We saw as much in the first chapters of the book of Job when the Lord's bold adversary incited the Lord to unleash evil upon a favored servant. The Lord doesn't just blast *that old serpent* out of the water because it would seem simpler to do so. Evil, no matter how unruly, must be allowed to trouble the world in God's cosmic project of love.

The moral of the story for us is that the Lord is not nearly as likely as we may have assumed to manipulate the world on our behalf. It's not that he can't. It's not that he never does manage the world in our favor. It's just that he is less likely to play favorites than we may have thought. Even his handpicked servants will often have to cope with the unruly forces of trouble. This concession of the Almighty to the forces of crime, sickness, and disaster in our world is truly the essential meaning of the book of Job. It's a concession of God that has pained many a believer.

Take my friend Al. Even from his birth, not even a Satan could successfully accuse the Lord of coddling him. Al

---

[*] Job 41:9.
[†] Job 41:34.

grew up with his parents, five siblings, and a good-sized extended family on a farm in Italy about forty-five miles east of Rome. As a barrel-chested, thick-necked, and ruddy teenager, he had already become accomplished at pruning vineyards with a simple knife and plowing wheat fields behind oxen mighty in brawn and odor. Then he got a message from his grandfather in America. A railroad company was willing to sponsor his immigration to upstate New York. With the promise of a dollar an hour in America instead of a dollar a day in Italy, the family shipped their oldest son across the Atlantic on the *Olympia* at the age of nineteen.

With only the beginnings of a formal education, Al did in America the only thing he knew, flex his knotty muscles. By the time he finished his working days, there wasn't a cushy month in his resume with two years in the railroad, a year in a casket factory, seven years in the city parks department, and seven years doing carpentry. He ended in the hardest, loudest, dirtiest job of all: fifteen years in a steel mill. Al calls his work at the steel mill "bull work." It seems life comes full circle. As a teen, Al drove the oxen; at the mill, Al worked like one. One ominous day in the steel mill ended Al's working days and began his "Job days"; that is, the days of his suffering like the Bible's hero Job. But we won't tell about that just yet.

Al married Marie at age twenty-four and began having a family of four children. All by the sweat of their brow they bought a house, improved it themselves, and kept a garden on their tiny Syracuse city lot complete with vegetables, herbs, cherries, a fig tree, citrus trees they brought in during the winter, and, of course, grapes. Al filled the freezer by hunting and fishing, and Marie filled the shelves by canning. Vacation meant packing the kids into the car and hitching up the pop-up trailer to head off for a week at one of the state parks. When Al was laid up for two weeks because of appendicitis, they had no savings or insurance to get them through. Even two weeks of lost work and the doctor bills threatened to put them so financially behind it might take years to recover, so hand-to-mouth was the family economy.

By now Al has become the most renowned storyteller in the church with his innumerable anecdotes about the farm in Italy, his working days, or his hunting escapades. But stories about the Lord's involvement in the first forty years of his life are meager. In fact, if someone were to search out the entire sea of humanity for a modern day Job, the supreme model of spiritual virtue, *blameless and upright, a man who fears God and shuns evil*, he probably would not pick out Al. Al would be the first one to admit it—or maybe the second, after Marie!

But Al does tell one story about a man, when Al was ten or eleven, who limped into town with a cane, his skin like a translucent film over his bones. The man was home after being a German prisoner during WW II. Al recalls his arrestingly good cheer. The man would forever sing wherever he was, he greeted everyone, he made spinning tops for children, and he proclaimed his message: "No one but the Lord saved me! Jesus kept me alive! That's right, *Jesus!*" For years the entire village talked admiringly of a run-in between "the Jesus-man" and the local priest, a notorious womanizer. "When we are born," said the poor man to the priest, "we are like donkeys. The Lord lets us have a long rope, so we can run wild and make asses of ourselves. But as life goes on, the Lord pulls in the rope bit by bit until we have to meet with him face to face." When the priest died after suffering a terrible sickness, the whole village recalled the Jesus-man's wisdom. Al the farm boy already knew a lot about stubborn donkeys, and the story about the Jesus-man and the priest made him wonder about his own meeting with the Lord someday.

As the years went by Al nearly forgot the Jesus-man. Heavenly-mindedness was simply not Al's particular distraction. For the next thirty years, if the knees on Al's pants were worn thin it was because of construction work, not praying. The soles of his feet and the palms of his hands were caked with the dirt of hard labor at work and around his home.

Even so, in the sixteenth year of their marriage with Al at the age of forty, Marie became a born-again Christian, and Al began considering in earnest the Lord's will for his life.

At first Al fought Marie about her conversion because he was more worried than impressed. He invited Marie's sister to the house to talk his wife out of her newfound faith. The sister shook the Bible at Marie: "You can't actually live by this, Marie!" Marie was undaunted. She continued to search for a church home, read her Bible, and listen to Christian teachings on tapes and the Christian radio station.

After a while, a new softness and gentleness about Marie struck Al as something real, blue-collar Christianity, not just high talk about a God no one could really understand anyway. Al knew that Marie had been toughened by the rough circumstances of her own life story. She had never been shown how to love others, but once she embraced Christ's love for her, she calmed down and began to have patience and sympathy she never had before.

In her new hunger for fellowship, Marie started hosting groups of believing friends at the house, and Al found himself surrounded by a shoulder-to-shoulder circle of enthusiasm for the things of another, invisible world. Once a visitor to one of Marie's home fellowships challenged him with Jesus' imperative: *"You must be born again."*[*] The challenge sounded like an ultimatum, and Al bristled at being handed an ultimatum within the walls of the home he had worked so hard for. The visitor pressed harder: "What if I'm right to believe, and you are wrong to fight it? You lose everything. But if I am wrong to believe, I haven't lost anything." Al ground the palms of his calloused hands together and thought of the transformation in his wife. The visitor was making sense.

Still there was one thing about Christianity that was intolerable to Al—*preaching*. He resented some lily white, soft-touched man, who didn't know strain and sweat, telling

---

[*] John 3:7.

him what to do. When Marie would play cassette tapes of sermons, he envisioned imperious dictators pointing bony fingers. When Marie finally settled down at Living Word Church, Al thought Marie's pastor, "Brother Bob," was some sort of pampered Mafioso figure. Tapes of his preaching so infuriated Al he wanted to choke someone. Al always referred disdainfully to her pastor as "your chief." Stretching his eyes wide for emphasis, he vowed to Marie that the next time he would be in a church it would be because someone was carrying him in his own casket.

At the time, Marie's church was about to pioneer its own academy, a Christian school for kindergarten through twelfth grade. Marie dreamed of pulling her two remaining school-aged children out of the public school, and enrolling them in Jesus' school. The tuition would tax the family's budget, and Al couldn't see paying for the kids' education when the public school was free. Marie was so insistent that she took a job cleaning houses to pay the tuition. Then she begged Al to go to a meeting at the church. There would be no sermons, she promised; it was only to be a question and answer period about the new school. Al felt like he needed to find out why Marie was so fired up about this school.

At the meeting Brother Bob walked by, and Marie elbowed Al and whispered, "There's *'your chief'*!" Al saw the preacher dressed in corduroys and a checked shirt covered with saw dust. Al heard him apologize to a small group of people nearby that he hadn't had time to change after cutting firewood for his woodstove. Al was close enough to smell the familiar gas/oil aroma of chainsaw work. Al's clenched fists and knotted jaw relaxed. Whatever was or was not said about the school that night was lost on Al. He was still dumb with surprise at the rough, unpretentious appearance of Marie's pastor.

The Lord finally made sense to Al when, alone in the bedroom one Sunday afternoon, he snuck a look at his wife's

King James Bible. He wanted to read a sentence or two from this "book of God" for himself. What was the great attraction?

He opened at random to the book of Hebrews and read, *But if ye be without chastisement, whereof all are partakers, then are ye bastards, and not sons.*[*] He was surprised to see the word *bastard* in the Bible. As a farmer, he understood there wasn't anything much lower on the pecking order than a bastard, a mutt. In his ethnic heritage an illegitimate child might be the one creature even a notch lower. He was surprised to see that the Bible contained such "country talk." He closed the book and decided he would read it again sometime.

The "again sometime" was only a minute later when he let Marie's Bible fall open again; it was the same page. He looked for a crease in the binding or waviness in the paper that would make the Bible open to that one spot. Nothing. He tried to get the gist of the entire verse this time: *But if ye be without chastisement, whereof all are partakers, then are ye bastards, and not sons.* He remembered how his father made him a good farmer by correcting him daily, usually many times a day. Al didn't usually mind it so much. He was proud of the farmer he had become. The Bible was right, getting chastised is part of being a real son.

He closed the Bible, waited only seconds this time, and flopped it open again. A third time the same spot. Al was not a complicated man, and for him three times was enough. Maybe he even *wanted* it to open to the same place three times. In any case, he was not about to question the Father's right to criticize his children, and he was sure he didn't want to be a bastard. As for preaching, if his heavenly Father wanted him to listen to preaching, he could do it. That night Al not only set foot in the church; he walked down the aisle to the front of the church, right in front of the whole crowd, and knelt and prayed and surrendered to Jesus.

---

[*] Hebrews 12:8.

Al only knew one way to serve the Lord. He wasn't going to be a preacher, teacher or a mighty prayer warrior. Regardless of his infinite supply of anecdotes from a colorful life, he wasn't the type to stand out in the crowd and prophesy great biblical truths and exhortations. But he could work with his hands. So he helped the men in the church remodel an old bus garage into classrooms for the new school. He also taught some young men in the church how to hunt and garden. He helped improve the church summer camp. All the work he had put toward scratching out a niche for himself, he now applied to helping the church. He felt that by helping the church, he was helping God.

More than ten years passed when one day at work in the steel mill, Al had to push a giant cylinder of solid steel, like a thick rod twelve inches in diameter and fourteen feet long, along a roller table to his powerful saw where he would cut the monster. It was the kind of work Al had been doing for fifteen years. He drove all his weight into the over-sized piece of steel to start it down the line. The cylinder got up some momentum with Al driving from behind almost like a football lineman, but for some reason it jammed on the rollers to a dead stop. The sudden stop caught him off-balance, and a strange twist felt like a lance drove up his back muscles to the shoulder. Pain drove him to his knees.

Later in the day, the company doctor examined him, and informed Al he had wrenched his back pretty severely, but the doctor was sure he would recover. Work in the mill was rough, and the doctor had seen a lot worse. Al would need some rest, he said. As it turned out, it was Al's last day on the job and the beginning of his own "trials of Job."

A patchy rash broke out on Al's face and chest, and flu-like symptoms flattened him while he was home trying to recover from his back injury. His muscles ached, his energy sagged, and he had a fever—strange back injury.

As the strength drained from Al's thick shoulders and neck over a period of weeks, doctors began a wide variety of tests. They eventually discovered Al to have a rare disease of the skin and muscles, *dermatomyositis*. Neither Al nor Marie would ever quite master the name of the disease, but they learned everything else about it, including that the disease often lasts a lifetime; it can kill.

Doctors don't understand why people come down with this disease in which the body's immune system attacks healthy muscle tissue. Some doctors believe that a trauma like Al experienced that day in the steel mill can trigger it. No matter the cause, the very muscles with which Al had built a life for his family and with which he now so happily served the Lord felt like sandbags. His diagnosis was only the beginning of the worst month of Al's life.

Marie's father died. Al and Marie may not have always had the model marriage, but one thing was for sure, they did everything together, especially since they had become Christians. But this time Al couldn't even get out of bed, so Marie was going to have to cope with her father's death practically without his support. Surely Marie didn't hold Al's sickness against him, but Al still felt like his inability to get out of bed was failure. That wasn't all, for the trouble was to come in waves.

In the same month, nightmarish news assailed their home. Their oldest son died in his home near Boston, MA. First reports that it was a suicide rocked Al and Marie. But some of the details didn't add up, and at least one lawman suspected foul play. Al was in no position to pester the law to re-investigate in a faraway city. He couldn't even attend his own son's funeral in Syracuse. He couldn't get his back off the bed.

To round out the month of misery Al's only daughter got mixed up in a relationship with a beast, and the relationship came to a violent crisis that month. All his life, Al had scratched out a life for himself by manual labor, and now he couldn't lift a fist to defend his daughter's honor. His daughter's abuse, his son's death, his wife's grief, his own illness—Al felt pinned under a pile-up, insult on top of injury.

The church prayed for Marie and the family; they prayed double for Al. In ten years of serving the Lord the couple had made themselves beloved to the church, and people came by the house to console them. Al and Marie both coveted the companionship and the prayer, and people did what they could—brought food, cleaned the house, ran some errands. People prayed and prayed. But the situation was awkward for Al. What could he say to describe his pain to people? Everyone felt helpless.

Even though Al had never been much of a philosopher or theologian, that didn't mean he didn't usually have plenty to talk about, at least a new story. Now it seemed strange that he was speechless. In his bed in a tiny front room of his little bungalow with some friends standing at bedside, Al expressed his suffering with an eloquent gesture instead. He would pull the sheet up over his face and weep. Only a Job could understand Al's pain: *"Why is light given to those in misery, and life to the bitter of soul, to those who long for death that does not come, who search for it more than for hidden treasure?"** Al says, like Job, he truly longed to die.

It's impossible to say just what part prayer played in Al's ordeal. He wasn't healed at the end of that terrible month. His disease might have killed him during the first two years, but it didn't. So maybe prayer helped keep him alive.

We know this: it has been almost twenty years now since Al had strength enough in his shoulders to take a plate down from the top shelf of the cupboard or in his legs to go down the basement stairs. He has had two heart attacks that the doctors know about. There have been countless falls, when his knees just buckled, and he would have to wait until someone heard his groaning or saw him and could pick him up. One winter night, he slipped on the snow by his front door and

---

* Job 3:20-21.

broke his leg in three places when his leg slipped under the porch railing. It almost killed him again with discouragement.

Even the efforts of the doctors were sometimes torturous, and Al jokes, "Doctors *practice* medicine. One day maybe they'll get it right." The physical therapy one doctor prescribed actually made the disease eat up his muscle mass faster. Another doctor prescribed steroids that turned him into a moody terror for the family and brought on diabetes. There were endless needle pricks for infusions, medicines, and tests. Finally Al made fourteen monthly trips to the National Naval Medical Center in Bethesda to play guinea pig in the test of a possible cure (Al was later told he was receiving the placebo for the first seven months).

In spite of the interminable ordeal something started happening inside Al. He began to "embrace the good." For instance, while at Bethesda, a world center for catastrophic illness and injury, Al saw whole hospital wings full of people in dire conditions: amputees, cancer patients, people who had radical brain operations. It reminded him that there were others worse off than him. He shouldn't complain.

On one visit to Bethesda for his "treatment" Al watched the eighteen-year-old girl across the hall who had to leave college because she also had Al's disease and was part of the experimental program. The girl's healthy sister was taunting her mercilessly by dancing around her. In anger, the invalid sprang off her couch and began dancing with twice the vigor of her tormentor. A minute into her gyrations, she threw herself into her family's arms and broke into joyful sobbing because she realized in that weird moment that her strength was returning. Al's disease is sometimes like that, as quick to retreat as it is to invade, and this young girl had just discovered she was in remission. Maybe the experimental medicine had worked. Al, too, cried like a baby as he watched from a distance. This pretty young girl, her whole life ahead of her, went into remission instead of him. He didn't want it any other way, so he wept with gratification.

Even the time Al broke his leg, and the pain and inconvenience assaulted his spirit, he eventually became infused with something good. His friends saw he needed to recuperate at home rather than in a dismal nursing home where ninety-nine percent of those admitted die, but there would be quite a challenge in caring for him at home. Who could daily lift him out of bed with his heavy cast? Marie couldn't do it. Al's health plan wouldn't cover the cost of a nurse.

Instead, a construction worker, a brother in Christ who would be off work for the winter months, volunteered. He came to Al and Marie's home every day, three times a day for over three months to get Al out of bed and bring him to the bathroom or hold him upright for a sponge bath. Three times a day. Every day. A smile, a greeting, and a grunt as he lifted Al. The brother's friendship, as well as that of the many other people who helped him, actually lifted Al's heart as well as his leaden flesh. The pain and inconvenience of his sickness and injury were awful, to be sure, but no suffering could spoil the preciousness of his friendships.

Al's ability to "embrace the good" grew out of his faith. In fact, faith enabled him not only to cope with the trial that never went away. Rather, Al's faith enabled him to *overcome* his trial. He trusted to his core, that however painful, inconvenient, and limited his life may have turned out, Jesus was with him. Al's faith is the reason he now tells the story of his life with the eagerness of a man who knows he is doing God's will. He has something to say, and he is not ashamed.

Al's muscle mass has slowly continued to waste away, so he can hardly testify of a miraculous recovery. In fact, to look at the way his skin drapes over his bones, he might remind us of the Jesus-man Al remembers from his childhood in Italy. Truly Al has now become the good-cheered Jesus-man. "Life with Jesus is good," Al tells people, undaunted by his trial. He says plainly that he does *not* want to die anymore. Coming from Al, such a confession is heavy with importance. Jesus has saved him, he says, and his role as a member in the body of

Christ is as dear to him as any man's might be. He again wants to live to the glory of God.

Not only can we now compare Al to the Jesus-man; we can also compare him, one more time, to the Bible's Job. Job's excruciating test ended. We read at the end of the Bible book that bears Job's name how the Lord *blessed the latter part of Job's life more than the first.*[*] His friends brought donations, and the Lord not only restored Job's wealth, he practically doubled it. Job even fathered a second family. The Bible especially highlights Job's three lovely young daughters who flitted around their father like so many birds, bringing comfort and pleasure to the noble elder. Job's new wealth and family represent the new life that God gives to those who overcome life's trials with their faith intact.

Now Al has attained the age, which in the Bible signifies the blessing of the Lord—seventy years old. At his seventieth birthday party, his children and grandchildren all hovered about him like the daughters of Job. By the scores, his friends gathered to give honor to the noble elder. His devoted son struggled through tears of love and admiration to offer prayer and praise to Jesus for his father. His daughter-in-law made a swelling speech. Surrounded by family and friends in the shade of a huge old maple tree on the lawn of his son's farm, Al was like the wise and tested biblical patriarch. Al's story is that of a man who has walked with God.

Al doesn't much care if he ever gets down into the basement again because he has a lot of other things to do. He has grandchildren he needs to take fishing or have to the house for weekend visits. He needs to help Marie cook special Italian dishes like no one else can. He needs to teach more of his friends how to prepare a fig tree for the cold Syracuse winter. He has to wander up and down the aisles

---

[*] Job 42:12.

of the farmer's market with his walker, so he can visit with his Italian compadres. The children at the church summer camp are counting on Al for rides in his golf cart. His nobility is an inspiration to all of us in the church as he joins us as often as he can, often two or three times a week, to praise the Lord. And his stories—we still don't think he has told them all.

## CHAPTER NINE

# The Refugee

*Matthew 15:25-28    The woman came and knelt before him. "Lord, help me!" she said.*
*He replied, "It is not right to take the children's bread and toss it to their dogs."*
*"Yes, Lord," she said, "but even the dogs eat the crumbs that fall from their masters' table."*
*Then Jesus answered, "Woman, you have great faith! Your request is granted." And her daughter was healed from that very hour.*

Jesus refused to heal this desperate woman's daughter at first because she was not Jewish. In fact, he suggested the woman was a dog because she was not Jewish. It may be hard for us to see Jesus' initial response to this poor soul as anything but mean.

If we can suspend our own cultural bias, some historical and cultural factors should soften our criticism. First, Jesus' response to the woman was an expected response in Bible days. Even though its connotation must have been insulting and no one, then or now, wants to be called a dog, it may help us to understand that "dog" was a common expression in the culture of Bible days for an unbeliever. We can paraphrase Jesus' response: "It is not right to give a believer's blessing to an unbeliever." Remarkably, this woman proved all cultural expectations wrong. She truly and deeply believed. She was not a dog after all. In fact, Jesus was about to both recognize and compliment her faith.

In addition, in biblical culture devout Jews stayed to themselves. Jesus in particular had an especially Jewish mission. He was the Jews' Messiah. He came to this world to fulfill the Jewish prophecies of the Jewish Bible. No doubt, the opportunity for salvation would also open to non-Jews in time, but the right time had not arrived yet. In other words, Jesus was on track. Healing this non-Jewish woman's daughter was not in keeping with Jesus' Bible-based mission as a fundamentally Jewish persona. Put plainly, Jesus' narrow focus prohibited him from helping this woman at first.

In the end though, the woman and her tormented daughter were more important to Jesus than any focus on his mission. He proved that if his role and his love came into conflict, his love held sway. He was not as obsessed with his role as he was obsessed with helping people. The story teaches us that hurting people down here can get the Lord's attention up there in heaven.

Getting God's disapproval with our sinfulness may be a given for most students of the Bible. Anyone with even a slight familiarity with the Bible can recall how God sent a great flood upon the earth in response to the world's wickedness or that God sent a rain of fire and brimstone upon Sodom and Gomorrah for theirs. A lot of people realize the Bible foretells a terrible Apocalypse in which the wrath of the Almighty sends woe after woe upon a world that has forgotten God. Even gentle Jesus taught about eternal judgment in hell more than anyone else in the Bible. What we may not realize equally is that the God of the Bible stands ready to reward faith. God may, in fact, change his mind about us if he sees our faith. We can impress the Lord with our faith!

In addition to the desperate woman who would be satisfied with Jesus' crumbs, King Hezekiah also changed his destiny because he believed. The prophet Isaiah predicted the great king's imminent death. But Hezekiah refused to lie down for this prediction of doom even though the prediction had come from a recognized seer. Rather he poured out his heart in prayer, requesting that the Lord would change his destiny. Before Isaiah could even depart from Hezekiah's palace, the Lord told the prophet to do an about-face. Hezekiah's cry of faith had changed the Lord's mind. The prophet was to inform Hezekiah that he would live another fifteen years.

The Lord may also respond to the acts of faith on a grand scale. In Jeremiah 26:3 the Lord said of wicked nations, *"Perhaps they will listen and each will turn from his evil way. Then I will relent and not bring on them the disaster I was planning because of the evil they have done."*

It's actually the exception in the Bible, not the rule, when the Lord closes the doors of destiny, locks them, and throws away the key. Rather, the Bible most often presents the future as unsettled, to be conditioned by man's response to the Word of the Lord. The Lord is waiting to see if we will respond to life's challenges with faith in him. Great predictions as well as great ordeals are chances to believe.

The woman in the Gospel of Matthew who would be satisfied with crumbs also proved something about herself, that she deserved high respect for *not* getting insulted or put off. The woman clung to Jesus because she understood an opportunity was passing. She wasn't about to let go. Her interesting combination of humility and audacity changed the Lord's mind about her. Her wisdom in responding mildly, cleverly, and positively got her daughter healed. Jesus himself would not mind stepping aside to allow the woman to take center stage—*"Woman, you have great faith!"* Faith had given dignity to the dog.


According to Mary, a friend in the church who came to Syracuse from war-torn southern Sudan, she was not kicked like a dog in her homeland. She was chased like a rat along with hundreds of thousands of other displaced Sudanese. Yet Mary changed her family's destiny when she turned to Jesus.

From her childhood through her teen years, Mary spent part of the year going to school in the southern Sudanese city of Bor and the rest of the year in nearby villages performing the Dinka tribe's traditional duties of herding cattle, sheep, and goats. Life in a *tookul*, a round grass hut with a conical roof, was primitive but peaceful. At seventeen Mary was wed to Akau, the young man her family had chosen for her. Akau was studying for a degree in agriculture and helping local herdsmen apply some modern techniques with their animals. In the second year of their marriage, Mary gave birth to a healthy daughter she named Gop. Life was good.

Peace and lofty dreams evaporated when Gop was fourteen months old and civil war exploded in Bor between Mary and Akau's black-skinned tribes of southern Sudan and the fairer, government-backed Muslim armies of the north. The Muslims, with superior weapons and training, sought to subjugate the civilian populations of the Dinka and Nuer tribes by shooting down their men with automatic weapons, raping their girls, stealing their livestock, and burning their homes.

As the armies from the north approached, millions of tribal people like Mary and Akau had to make hurried live-or-die decisions. Mary and Akau decided to join the massive flow of refugees that was fleeing to Ethiopia from the cruel advance of the Muslims. But they hedged their bet. Fearing they might be killed on the run and hoping soldiers wouldn't be much interested in either a baby or an old lady, they left Gop behind with Akau's mother. At least their daughter might save the family line from utter elimination.

Mary and Akau walked day and night to stay ahead of their persecutors. They would allow themselves no more than a couple hours of sleep each night. There were thousands of people ahead of them and behind them. Most of fugitives were young boys the rest of the world nicknamed "The Lost Boys" after Peter Pan's inner circle of devotees. It was a human column of primal terror, the perfect target for their tormentors' crossfire.

No matter how much Akau urged Mary to rest she refused. Terror's adrenalin empowered her to flee without flagging. They would only risk tiny sips of water from their gourd bottle, not knowing when they might replenish their supply. They carefully avoided watering holes, fearing that the enemy soldiers would wait for them there with automatic weapons.

Mary and Akau witnessed many people fainting on the edge of the road from dehydration, the weak ones who would then become easy prey for jackals and lions. When the water in their gourd ran out, Mary literally shook when they approached a well-known oasis and weighed their choices: death by rifle fire or death by jackals and lions. The only consolation Akau could offer was that they had indeed made the best decision to leave Gop with his mother. To their surprise, they filled their gourd and stole away unchallenged.

When the column of escapees finally did reach water in abundance, it meant tragedy rather than relief. The River Gilo, several hundred feet wide, barred their advance. Few of the Sudanese children knew how to swim, and River Gilo's banks were the home of crocodiles. Even so the escapees, like a column of rats, pushed forward in desperate flight from the soldiers that were attacking at the rear. Mary saw many young boys taken under by the swift currents while some others, pushed on makeshift rafts by their older brothers, scanned about in wide-eyed desperation. She was thankful she could swim until she saw crocodile attacks churn the otherwise even surface of the water. When she was half way across the river she spotted the scaly backbone of one crocodile breaking water beside her as it glided past.

In their little corner of this civil war Mary and Akau were particles in a river of humanity winding across two hundred miles of Sub-Saharan desert over a period of several weeks. The greater war lasted from 1983 until 1998 and displaced an estimated 4.5 million Sudanese. It's guessed that the war caused 1.9 million deaths. It was the greatest loss of life by war in the world during the last two decades of the twentieth century.

In 1986, along with Mary and Akau, about 26,000 Dinka and Nuer people left the vicinity of Bor city. Someone at the head of the line had the idea to flee to Ethiopia and was able to somehow spread word through the crowd. Ethiopia had soldiers at their border. They would protect the refugees. Along the way, a man would be posted here and there to prod the people forward, "Keep going. God will help you!"

There were enough refugees from the Bor region, and their story of flight to Ethiopia was so hair-raising, the world noticed and sent U.N. and Red Cross airdrops of essential aid near the border of Sudan and Ethiopia. A small staff of U.N. social workers tried to bring order and hygiene into the camps just across the border. When U.N. personnel insisted that the women and men be separated into different camps, Akau informed Mary that he was going back to Bor to join the Sudanese People's Liberation Army in the fight for a homeland against the raiders from the north. Mary was not to see Akau for over two years, not until she decided to go back to Bor herself to fetch her daughter Gop.

Mary became encouraged to leave the relative safety of a refugee camp and walk the two hundred miles back to Bor for Gop because she was hearing that the Muslim forces had lost interest in the city after so humiliating it. More importantly, she was having terrible dreams about Gop being killed at the hands of the attackers.

Amazingly, on the way back, Mary found Akau at a camp and spent two days with him before they continued their separate parts of the battle to survive. They discussed that Akau might come to see her and Gop, but it might not be for a while. Nine months later, Akau's mother performed the services of a midwife as Mary gave birth to their second daughter Abiei in a village near Bor. Akau was good to his word; he came home when Abiei was one and beginning to walk.

The little family was together for two months when the Muslim armies began tormenting Bor again, this time with artillery and air attack. When the bombs began to fall, Akau would shoo his little family, like so many rats, into the shelter of holes the village people had carved out of the ground and covered with heavy wood. Inside the holes, just big enough for four or six people, Mary would shake like she had two years before near the oasis, and plead to the heavens for the Muslims to stop. Gop, five years old by then, would become indignant, "Why are you so scared, Mommy? They are people, not animals. They won't hurt us." Little did she know. Many of the neighbors who balked at the humiliation of climbing into those holes lost their lives in the attacks.

One day reports came that the dreaded ground troops were sweeping through the city. Mary heard automatic gunfire and began a hurried escape with the children. Akau remained to cover their backs and delay the advance of the Muslim troops. It was the last time Mary was ever to see her city or her husband. She later learned the raiders shot and killed her husband.

The Dinka custom was for the dead husband's brother to care for the widow and father children to carry on the dead brother's legacy, so Mary moved in with Akau's brother in a village that had thus far been uninteresting to the Muslims, Kapoita. Mary would live there for two years and become pregnant with her third child. Then the chase began again.

One night in Kapoita, Mary had the same dream two times in one night. A voice told her, "Mary, run now! Go this way!" and she would see, like in a video game, a winding path appear through the village past some familiar landmarks. Early the next morning she pleaded with her brother-in-law to gather some belongings and head out of the village. She was sure her dream meant soldiers were coming.

They argued, the brother-in-law thinking the dreams were groundless. The entire household pressured Mary to cease her hysteria, but Mary would have none of it. She harnessed baby Abiei in a sling on her back, took Gop by the hand, and pregnant as she was, headed for the desert at eight in the morning.

At midnight that night the sweep of Muslim soldiers did indeed surprise the town with a brutal purge. Mary's relatives managed to leave the village with only moments to spare, death-screams in their ears. They would catch up with Mary in a few days.

The new destination: Kenya. They headed for the refugee camp called Kakuma, which by now had become home to 10,000 of the Lost Boys of the Dinka tribe plus over 20,000 other refugees from neighboring regions. Once again a refugee camp was no place for a woman, so the men of Mary's extended family bussed her and her children to housing projects in Nairobi, Kenya.

Mary's eight years in Nairobi dulled into a grind, a welcome grind because having to chase down a cheaper place to live or a sewing chore by which to earn some change was better than being chased by rifle-wielding terror-mongers. Mary gave birth to Deng, her first son, and her brother-in-law also joined them for five of those eight years. Mary had one more of each, a daughter Athok and a son Ayuen.

In Nairobi Mary befriended three women, a little circle of comfort, who introduced her to a vivid Christianity she had not known before. The four of them would often gather in one of their homes to raise such a commotion in prayer as to match the most heated revival meeting. True to the revival tradition, some of their prayer sessions ended with an invitation for Mary to accept Jesus as her personal Savior. She loved her friends, and she loved their times of fervent prayer. But strangely, she refused her friends' invitation every time.

To a person in Mary's war-ravaged world, a commitment to Christ could mean violating the first principle of survival: never allow yourself to get cornered. Always be ready to flee. Maintain your independence. So Mary could pray with her friends and cry out to Jesus with the fire of a mystic, she could relish their comfort and friendship, but she refused to join them in their church. She had never surrendered to anyone or anything. How could she surrender to Jesus?

As each of the women entered the United Nations' refugee resettlement program, Mary's circle of comfort began to dissolve. The U. N. High Commissioner of Refugees was sending Mary's friends to Australia. Mary and her five children were headed to Connecticut. Her brother-in-law would stay in Kenya. When tears streamed down Mary's high cheekbones, her friends would prop up her spirits. "Mary, let God choose. Let him take care of you."

Mary didn't let herself believe it. Why would God trouble himself with a rodent? But Mary was never able to forget one of her friend's parting advice: "Always pray, Mary."

The separation from her Christian prayer partners meant Mary arrived in America despairing. From her arrival at John F. Kennedy International Airport to the church that sponsored her resettlement, every impression of life in America unnerved her: escalators that seemed like people-grinding monsters; black men with dread locks and clownish jeans hanging low on their rears; somber church services that were scripted by antique rituals; and a cost of living in Connecticut destined to ruin her. A feeling swept over her that she should flee back to ghettos of Nairobi with her children where she might at least fight for survival on a familiar battleground. As she contemplated an escape back to the rat's life, she recalled the voice of her friend: "Always pray, Mary."

In her over-priced apartment Mary dropped to her knees. "Lord, I can find you anywhere, in a shack if I have to, but my children, Lord. Protect my children." The Lord's answer would come by bits, like crumbs gathered from under the table. Literally, it started with some strange phone calls.

Mary only spoke a few words of English when the phone first rang with a call from a woman in Syracuse, NY. Mary handed the phone to Gop whose English was better because of the schools in Nairobi. After a few words, Gop handed the phone back. The woman's name was Linda, and she was calling because she heard about Mary from some Sudanese Lost Boys in Syracuse. Gop said that Linda insisted on talking to Mary. Mary took the phone and listened to the babble in her earpiece. She could only make out a word here and there, *home, love, family, pray, Jesus.* At least they were good words.

For the first few calls from Linda, Mary and Gop would play their game of hot potato with the phone, but somehow Mary always lost the game. Linda made sure the phone always ended in Mary's hands. The better Mary's English became, the less she would hand the phone to Gop and the better she realized Linda was her Christian friend like her friends back in Nairobi who she missed so dearly. Too bad Linda lived so far away.

In time Linda, her husband, and another couple visited Mary in Connecticut; then Mary got her chance to visit Syracuse. It turned out Mary had a long lost cousin that lived in Syracuse and also knew Linda and her husband. He offered to pick up Mary and the children and bring them to Syracuse. Mary still didn't feel ready to trust anyone or try to make a connection in America because she felt so alienated, but she mustered the resolve to make the trip. By the time the compact car, packed with a collection of the darkest-skinned, whitest-eyed faces on the road that night, arrived at Linda's it was after 4:00 Saturday morning.

Just the same, when the door of Linda's house opened, the little crowd gathered inside, both Americans and Dinkas from the Syracuse area, let out a cry of welcome. There were hugs and hearty handshakes, and platters of eggs, bagels, fruits and cheese. Best of all there was uplifting talk and Mary's special love—loud, heartfelt prayer. Before the visitors from

Connecticut would be allowed to sleep there was yet to be a full day of celebrations with a full contingency of Mary's compatriots from Sudan. Towards the end of the day Linda cornered Mary with an invitation to church on Sunday morning.

The invitation made Mary feel wonderfully like she had when her friends in Nairobi used to invite her to their church. She had always refused them. She had tenaciously protected her independence in her effort to stay unconnected and agile. Cut, run, live another day—it was the survivor's creed. But Linda's invitation was a chance to embrace a new life. Maybe Mary wasn't destined to play this role of lonely fugitive after all. The children needed a home. Mary agreed to come to church.

It had been a long time since Mary felt so happy with expectation as she did on the way to church that morning. She wasn't disappointed. The church people had a clean, neat appearance. Many of the men wore ties, and all the women wore skirts. It seemed right to her, wholesome. When the service started the room filled with the sound of God's people praying, singing, clapping, and worshiping. People gathered by the scores at the front of the church to pray with each other.

At the end of the sermon the preacher invited hungry souls to come down the aisles to receive Christ as Savior. Linda, seated next to Mary, asked, "Do you want to go up front and give your heart to Jesus, Mary?"

The advice of her friend back in Nairobi echoed in her ear: "Let God take care of you." Part of Mary wanted to cut and run as she had learned to do whenever she felt cornered. Another urge inside her beckoned her forth from the camps and ghettos, from the war, from the hard customs of Africa, from fleeing any more.

Like the woman in the Bible that would be satisfied with crumbs, Mary wasn't going to let Jesus pass by her this time. Mary, bowed over with sobbing, had to have Linda's help to make it to the front of the church. It was nothing new for Mary to drop to her knees and raise her hands, every finger like a ray extending toward heaven. She prayed, the tears streaming down her black cheeks and dripping from her chin. But the prayer itself was indeed new and liberating. "I don't want to lead myself any more, Lord. Jesus, you lead me. I am yours," she cried in her native tongue.

Mary knew the Lord had brought her to a special place, so when it was almost time to stop praying she added, "If this place is to be my church show me, Lord Jesus, and these people will be my people forever." As Mary prayed she closed her eyes and saw an image of a strange *tookul* like the round grass hut with the conical roof that so symbolized the peace and safety of her early life. Only it was made of modern, shiny materials instead of grass. She didn't understand.

Nevertheless, it was an exhilarating time of decision, humility, release, and comfort for her. The Lord had communed with her, as she had never experienced in her life. The morning service ended while Mary basked in the radiance of Jesus' love and acceptance and met so many enthusiastic new friends.

After church, Mary and a dozen or so people meandered out to the parking lot on their way to Sunday dinner before driving back to Connecticut. Mary turned to get a last look at the church building that housed the wondrous events of that morning. She was astonished. There it was! On the top of the large auditorium roof, there was a cupola Mary had not noticed when they arrived that morning. The cupola was round and had a conical roof. Since the church building was large, the cupola itself was as big as a hut. Actually it was about the same size and shape as a Dinka *tookul*. Mary then knew what the image of the *tookul* meant that she saw during prayer that morning. This house of worship was to be her and her children's refuge. The people of this house were her family, her people.

A Psalm expresses an oft-repeated promise in the Bible: *The LORD watches over the alien and sustains the* *fatherless and the widow.*[*] Mary believes with all her heart that the Lord did exactly so with her and her children. He kept them in the desert. He helped them escape their attackers. He brought them safely to the US. He led a Christian woman to call and call and never give up. Someone even bought a house in Syracuse especially for Mary, so she could live in a neighborhood safe for her children. Someone else has paid for her school-aged children to go to a private Christian school. In fact, Abiei graduated from Living Word Academy last year. Now Mary's Abiei and Gop are both in college. Mary has a full-time job. She has more friends than ever with which to pray her heart out.

We may wonder, if the Lord is the sustainer of the alien, the fatherless, and the widow, why he ever let them become such. Wouldn't it have been better if the Lord protected them from such destitution in the first place? Actually, the situation of the alien, the fatherless and the widow is the perfect metaphor for the lesson of this book. God, in truth, does not often intervene to stop the innocent from becoming refugees, widows, or orphans. It's so because he has created a free world in which there is a great deal of grief and evil, as we have explored already in many other chapters. What happens in response to an ordeal then becomes the key.

Will the needy soul turn to the Lord in his ordeal, so the Lord can show himself as the Sustainer? Will that needy soul persevere beyond insult, discouragement, and alienation to touch the Lord's heart? The woman who told Jesus she was willing to eat crumbs did. So did Mary.

---

[*] Psalm 146:9.

## CHAPTER TEN

# The Alcoholic

*Romans 8:8-9 Those controlled by the sinful nature cannot please God. You, however, are controlled not by the sinful nature but by the Spirit, if the Spirit of God lives in you.*

Laboratory science, from the first systematic dissections of cadavers in the mid-nineteenth century to the Human Genome Project, has taught us a lot about what's going on in the body when well or ill, gifted or disabled. Our ever-increasing understanding has already enabled us to immunize vast populations against the likes of polio, measles, and smallpox. Modern medicines have brought other once-rampant infections, including tuberculosis, gonorrhea, and malaria, under control in many or most places. Because of our growing knowledge we have a fighting chance for long, productive lives in the face of once-unassailable diseases such as some cancers, heart disease, diabetes, and others. There is encouraging science in the fight against HIV/AIDS.

Not only has our American judicial system learned to use our DNA to connect our family lines. We have also learned that DNA encodes our eye color, our tendency toward high cholesterol, our life expectancy, and perhaps even whether we are cheery or blue. The study of DNA has led us to cell therapy, which may in the future provide dramatic cures of such maladies as cancer, kidney disease, and catastrophic spinal cord damage. In short, we live at a time blessed with

unprecedented understanding, a quickly expanding understanding, of why we are the way we are and how to improve
our prospects for a long, productive life.

The advances of health science help put God, Satan,
and suffering in their proper relation. Mostly, the more science
explains about why we are sick and handicapped, the less likely
we will be to blame our physical maladies on God (or Satan).
For instance, we thank the Lord that better health care has
steadily increased the average lifespan of people in the
civilized world since the advent of laboratory science. It would
be silly, however—maybe *superstitious* is a better word for
it—to claim the shorter lives of earlier generations were simply
the will of God. Better health care has not suddenly changed
the will of God (or Satan) for how long most people should
live.

The more biotechnology can eliminate our suffering,
the less completely we will rely on the Lord to intervene when
we need fixing. Our self-reliance is probably all right with the
Lord because he would *want* us to take advantage of many of
the modern advances in the science of healing. The ethical
quagmires of biotechnology aside (such as those connected
with the use of mood-enhancing drugs, cloning, the sources for
stem cells, etc.), why wouldn't the Lord want us to be diligent,
responsible, and smart about making the world a better place
through at least some kinds of scientific research? We have a
God-given responsibility to improve the world. He doesn't
want us to be shirkers of this responsibility in the name of
piety. I certainly wouldn't want to eliminate modern biotechnology just so we could have a better chance at learning
"pure faith."

For the purposes of this book we need to consider that
advances in medical science seem like part of a pattern that is
almost intoxicating in its implications—we only have to keep
learning why we are the way we are so we can heal ourselves,
perhaps even enhance ourselves more to our liking. Learn-
heal-enhance—will we discover the fountain of youth if we just

keep learning? Genetic engineering, chemical enhancement, prosthetics—what might the studies of the coming century make possible? What does any of this say about God? To answer we have to realize that patterns rarely extend without end, and the learn-heal-enhance pattern will someday hit a wall.

The hope that medical science will create heaven on earth is still the stuff of science fiction. According to the President's Council on Bioethics in 2003, the day when genetic engineering can fabricate a single human strong in body, noble in mind, and upright in spirit is not even on the horizon. Let alone engineering our way to a fair and loving mankind!

Even in an unlikely future when we attain the know-how to engineer one super human, we would have the insurmountable problem of distributing new technology fairly to all, especially to the poor. Scary thought for a science-fiction novel: only the rich could afford "super-babies." Even scarier thought because we can read about it in our newspapers and journals right now: advances in biotechnology may already be making the world *less* fair.

For example, most of the approximately 1.2 million Americans with HIV/AIDS have liberal access to many of the latest treatments, which both lengthen life expectancy and improve quality of life. On the other hand, over 25 million people with HIV/AIDS in Sub-Saharan Africa do *not* have this access because they are very poor. This is not to pretend access to treatments *within* the US is equal from wealthy victims to poor. In fact, inequity in the US only further confirms that our world faces some daunting social problems. It seems like political and social isolationism is bound to take its toll on the disadvantaged in this world.

The point is, we will always need God. Our scientific advancements are not going to squeeze God off his throne. Our limitations, whether social, political, or technical, leave a pit of need in our world that only the Almighty can fill. It's indeed *still* right and *still* healthy to feel our need for heaven's intervention. Since it's good to humble ourselves in the sight of the Almighty, however smart and able we become, let's turn to the Bible.

Readers of the Bible should not think it strange that biological science increasingly finds hormones, genetics, our central nervous systems, nutrition, our environments, and a host of other biological factors and systems help create powerful urges from our dark sides. There is really no discord between the ideas of scientific determinations and biblical determinations of our behavior. The Bible plainly recognizes the influence of our bodies in making us who we are, only the Bible usually refers to our biological systems as our *flesh* generally instead of using today's ultra-specific scientific explanations. The Bible, in fact, binds a proper understanding of our fleshly nature with our sinfulness.

The flesh, according to the Bible, is the part of any person that makes him act irrationally, a lot like an animal. It makes us pant for sex, pay a ridiculously high price for fun, and fight for territory simply to satisfy the urge to dominate. It's the part of us that modern advertisers have learned to exploit—our animal hot buttons—so we will "Just do it" (Read: Just *buy* it).

Here are some of the Bible's statements about the flesh:

- *I see another law at work in the members of my flesh, waging war against the law of my mind and making me a prisoner of the law of sin at work within my members.*[*]
- *I know that in me (that is, in my flesh,) dwelleth no good thing: for to will is present with me; but how to perform that which is good I find not.*[†]
- *"The spirit is willing, but the flesh is weak."*[‡]

---

[*] Romans 7:23.
[†] Romans 7:18 (King James Version).
[‡] Matthew 26:41 (King James Version).

Interestingly, centuries before we began disemboweling bodies in laboratories, Jesus and the writers of the Bible described us in real trouble as a result of our biological urges!

This is not to say that every urge of our flesh is sinful. The Lord after all, did tell the first husband Adam and wife Eve to be fruitful and multiply! But since Adam, sin has also been the natural imperative of our flesh, and there is no vaccine known to man that can immunize us against the sickening effect of sin's infection. In fact, if we stop reading the Bible after the few verses above, we seem biblically, as well as scientifically, bound to act like animals. But let's not stop reading...

> *For if you live according to the sinful nature, you will die; but if by the Spirit you put to death the misdeeds of the body, you will live, because those who are led by the Spirit of God are sons of God.* [*]

In other words, the work of God's Spirit within God's children is so empowering we can overcome our fleshly or sinful urges, so we can spiritually live. The reference in this passage to living is not to future eternal life with God in heaven. It refers to possessing spiritual vitality in our present experience. With the Spirit's help, it's possible to conduct ourselves like the special creation the Lord intended us to be rather than like animals bound by instinct. Modern advertising strategies, thankfully, don't have the last word on human behavior. We are not, when following the Lord, bound to live a reptilian, strike-on-impulse existence.

If the best measure of a victory is the strength of the opponent, my friend Scott's battle with his fleshly nature was a

---

[*] Romans 8:13-14.

notable proving ground for the power of God's Spirit. Specifically, Scott was mentally, emotionally, and physically addicted to drugs, booze, and anger. Since he began drinking his first hard liquor and sniffing his first glue at the awkward age of eleven, we hesitate to think of him as responsible for his behavior. We want to think his problems were simply the unavoidable outcome of nature and nurture. Of course, in case some combination of nature and nurture doesn't explain his problems fully, we might just have to throw into the mix some plain ol' knuckle-headedness.

As for nature: Some people suspect the tendency toward substance abuse is "in the blood." If so, Scott had an excellent pedigree. He was in a line of alcoholics that stretched before him at least two generations on his mother's side. If a scientist wants to find a booze-gene, Scott's DNA would make rich hunting ground.

And nurture: Scott grew up in a town so far north in New York, it borders on Canada. It seems like the town met the challenge to keep warm in the winter with hard liquor because it boasted more than its share of drinking joints and liquor stores, at least an even ten, for the 8000 year-round inhabitants. His parents were avid customers.

Scott's mother was a quart-a-day-of-vodka alcoholic, who daily began drinking before she was out of her bedclothes. His father was more the bar-type of slosher. When his parents were both home the chemistry was volatile. A family dinner put the whole table setting at risk because an argument was likely to have the dishes flying before the meal was done. But not to worry for the china overmuch, family warring made family dinners uncommon. When Scott was eleven, he spent most of his summer and early fall nights in the woods or on the streets. Sleeping in a perch up in a tree or inside a dumpster lined with rags was more comfortable than a softer bed in a war zone.

Finally, knuckle-headedness: Scott had his chances to turn to the good. For instance, he might have embraced the neighbors who felt sympathy for him as a kid and brought him along with their family to the local fairs or for a ride in a fire truck. Or there were the several chances Scott had to live with his sister and brother-in-law. They were stable people who were willing to help out a younger brother if only he would take root with them. Even in school, Scott never forgot how one teacher, seeing a bright kid battling with his dark side, told him the future was his for the choosing: the Presidency or prison. At sixteen when Scott moved in with his father who had remarried and moved to Syracuse, he had his last best run at President with a fresh beginning in a new school. Scott treated this chance the way he had treated all the previous ones. He knocked it to the side. Pained as he was, Scott preferred loneliness. He attended ninth grade only one day before deciding to quit school forever.

There was one night, back when Scott was eleven and walking the streets, that puts Scott's entire childhood into perspective. He stopped to gaze through the picture window of a schoolmate's house. He wondered at the scene, the boy seated with his family in their living room, bathed in golden light, giggling and talking. To Scott it was like looking through a magic portal into a make-believe world where there was peace. He was sure such peace was never to be his.

By the time Scott quit school he had already been a glue-sniffing, whiskey-drinking, pot-smoking, drug-running vagabond for five years. For the next two years, anything he cared about fit in his knapsack, and he took to the road bouncing between North Country towns and Syracuse. In fact, his whole life became a pattern of bounces: employment—hired then fired; jail—in then out; drug abuse—high then low; a valid driver's license—yes then no. The more freedom he had the more it seemed like the only thing that came naturally to him was mayhem.

There are a lot of ways we can measure the might of substance abuse's grip on Scott. As for his alcoholism, he started stealing a quart of whiskey a day from a liquor store.

As a drug-abuser, he graduated from pot to popping hallucinogens, to shooting coke, to robbing a pharmacy. As for other crime, he once got a month in jail for trying to steal a car without a transmission in it. The justice of the peace of his hometown ordered that if Scott ever set foot in the town again he would be arrested on the spot and sent to the slammer.

One night when he was in a cabin in the Adirondacks with his cronies, he drank a concoction someone called "ginseng tea." His buddies claimed that over the next hours he was howling at the moon and darting through the woods like a wolf. He never came in that night, but his buddies didn't even contact any authorities. A State Trooper stumbled upon him two days later walking aimlessly along a dirt road, naked, bloody, hypothermic, and out of his mind. Scott spent three days in a hospital recovering.

Around the time of the "tea" incident, Scott had enough sense left to pray for the first time in his life: "God, send me a girlfriend." It might have been a turn toward the good for Scott, even if it only meant that he didn't want to be alone any more. The girlfriend Jean didn't much seem like an answer to prayer at first since she was quite the junkie herself, but someday she was indeed to become a key to Scott's deliverance from all that bound him. Scott appeared before a justice of the peace again, this time to marry Jean in June of 1975, shortly after they realized Jean was pregnant.

One might expect the Lord could use marriage and their first child to induce some sobriety into Scott's and Jean's lives. Jean was indeed careful not to abuse drugs and booze while she was pregnant. Scott simply carried on as ever. And once their little girl was born healthy, Jean simply rejoined her husband in their dissipation. A lasting turn for the good was still, unfortunately, about nine years off.

Backtracking to the time of Scott's prayer for a girlfriend, it was also about then that Jean's brother Eddie committed his life to Christ. At first Scott and Jean thought Eddie had cracked up. How nutty Eddie was to immerse himself in reading the Bible, as if his life depended on it! He completely changed his lifestyle and friends. He was going to church many times a week. As ironic as it sounds, Scott and Jean talked over the prospects for kidnapping Eddie from the strange cult that had captivated him. They could de-program him, they thought, and get him back on party-track. They got even more concerned when they snuck into the basement to spend a night together only to wake up and find Eddie praying near their feet. They had never before heard such energetic, earnest, long prayer. Eddie was so lost in prayer he never even knew they were there.

Eddie made his sister's conversion a personal priority, but he wasn't the preaching type. He treated her warmly, gave her money when she was destitute, and did chores for her like painting the house Jean's parents had provided for Jean, Scott, and the baby. In short, he never refused a call for help. Over the eight years between Eddie coming to Christ and the day Jean finally believed too, Eddie would often do Scott's chores while Scott was in jail or a rehab facility.

Meanwhile, the stakes for Scott's behavior got higher. Scott was often unemployed, putting the new family on the financial good graces of Jean's parents. He even squandered their support. At the same time, he accumulated DWI charges, and his jail sentences got longer. Behind him was a trail of arrests, fights, injuries, wrecked cars, lost jobs, and unpaid bills. Scott became physically and verbally abusive with Jean. Higher stakes didn't bring about greater self-control, and Jean just seemed to get used to the hell on earth they had created together.

It wasn't that they couldn't recognize their lives were out of control. They saw how Scott's best buddy died in a motorcycle accident. Another pal burned to death in a house fire, probably because he was insensible, in the stupor of booze or drugs. Scott and Jean well-understood Scott's choices had been pared to a minimum: death, prison, or change. One time Scott was forced into a rehab program by the courts. Another time the two of them volunteered for a program together as an addict and a co-dependent. Still chaos seemed to rule their lives. For instance, Scott stopped drinking during one term in a rehab program, but incredibly, the same night he was released, he injected coke into his veins for the first time in his life. If ever a man was programmed to abuse himself!

In the eighth year of their marriage and with two children by then, Jean had enough. She didn't leave Scott; she turned to Jesus. Eddie's kindness, gentleness, and steadiness got to her. Eddie had peace; Jean, confusion. Eddie had wholesomeness; Jean, vulgarity. Eddie finished college; Jean quit high school. She finally admitted to herself that the difference was Jesus. It didn't much matter to her if anyone, Scott included, might ridicule her for turning to Jesus. Either her brother Eddie wasn't so deranged after all, or if someone preferred to think of it the other way, she was finally willing to join her brother in nuttiness. It couldn't be a turn for the worse, as far as Jean was concerned.

Some Christians talk about a "honeymoon with the Lord." It's a period when the new Christian's elation makes it easy and fresh to accept the faith's new lifestyle. Scott says that when Jean sobered up and embraced the Christian values of kindness, honesty, and service, he got the honeymoon. During the first year of Jean's salvation Scott cut back on his use of drugs and alcohol. He began a career for the first time in his life as an apprentice to become a professional heavy equipment operator. Jean gladly drove him to and from work every day. They stopped fighting, and started aiming for some long-term goals like getting Scott's driver's license back and buying a home. Unfortunately, honeymoons end.

Earning the best wages of his life and having purchased a house for the first time in their marriage, Scott got cocky and restless. At first he started picking on Jean for going to church. Then he started getting violent again, throwing her Bible across the room, screaming, "How can you believe that!" or blocking her exit from the house when she wanted to go to church, "Leave that church, so we can live like everyone else again."

For the next ten years Jean met her husband's opposition with increasing determination to serve the Lord. Eventually they had a third child, and she summoned the courage to enroll all three of their children in Living Word Academy. She couldn't afford the tuition, but the church accepted the children on a special arrangement, and she took some babysitting jobs to contribute at least a few dollars towards tuition and pay for gas to get the children to and from school. Because her relationship with Scott was so rocky, she also started nursing school to gain a good paying career with which to support herself and the children during the inevitable emergency. In spite of Scott's opposition, the plan was working, and their oldest daughter eventually graduated from Living Word Academy and was starting college.

Then Scott got a job out of town on a pipeline project, and something snapped. He had started sleeping at the jobsite, and before long, he resumed his binge drinking. Scott's former habits were back with a vengeance, and Jean began to bear the old brunt. But her old tolerance for Scott's excess was gone now that she had a few dollars in her purse from nursing work. She felt backed up against the impossibility of seeing Scott reform, while at the same time, the soap-opera side of the medical profession in a big hospital was alluring. Scott finally got the ungodly desire he had worked so hard for. Jean forsook Jesus and her lifestyle of faith. But he also lost. Jean wanted nothing to do with him. She demanded they separate. Scott moved out humiliated.

Strangely, Scott saw something like a valve at work in Jean's life, at first allowing a great flow from one source and then, with a twist, allowing a rush from a second source. The flow of goodness that had immersed their home when Jean was serving the Lord dried up when Jean left the Lord. A new wave of binges, needles, altercations, and wrangles with the law came in like a flood. For Scott it was like coming full circle back to his drunken, warring childhood home. The blank look in his youngest boy's eyes was strangely reminiscent of the hopeless look in his own eyes when he was a boy.

Witnessing first hand the switch in his wife—from the godless junkie during the first nine years of their marriage to the Christian saint in the second nine and then back again—was enough to crack Scott's sin-hardened heart. Scott had no doubts anymore that there must be a source of awesome power behind that switch. He knew he needed that power, but, as always, he found it difficult to reach out.

Strung out by drug and alcohol binges and lonely hours of humiliation and fruitless soul-searching, a crack became a total breakdown and made Scott desperate. Scott felt like he was about to be swept over an edge into destruction. A phone call to Jean was a last handhold. She had never before heard such a deep sense of defeat in Scott's tone. Her medical training enabled her to see the urgency of Scott's condition, so, in spite of her loathing, she rushed to the apartment he had taken during their separation.

Scott was a tormented beast. His inner person could no longer bear the thirty-eight years of abuse and anger. Psychologically, Scott was stretched as emotionally tight as a life of homelessness and running could make him. Pathologically his substance abuse over-taxed his senses but dulled his mind. Fearsome images and voices swirled and blurred the line between the real and the imagined.

With just the two of them in Scott's apartment, he pulled a knife on Jean, the person that had humiliated him. He threatened to kill her because she had spurned him, preferring the hospital crowd. "Get out of my life!" he cried. No, Scott thought, that's the devil's voice. He realized she was now also the one person in the world with a hand still out, so to save her, he locked himself in the bathroom. "I'll just kill myself, Jean. I don't want to live any more. There's no place for me here. I ruin everything I touch."

Jean could not have been more terrorized if she was on the knife-edged ridge of a Himalayan mountain. But she realized if she ran, Scott might carry through his plan. She talked him down from his hysteria and out of the bathroom, down the flight of stairs and out to the car. She sped him to the hospital, taking every turn feeling as though something volatile was about to spill and flash into an inferno. The next thing Scott remembers was waking up in a hospital room, his arms and legs strapped to the table.

As a result of that hellish night, Scott volunteered to check into the Tully Hill Treatment Center for a thirty-five day stay, but he also knew from past experience that the well-meaning program would not free him from the demons that so haunted him all his life. He had not forgotten the valve in Jean's life, the way it had so perfectly demonstrated that the power of heaven could make a person new. With one desperate effort he reached for the one hand strong enough to pull him out of his bondage. It was the same hand that had brought him Jean when he prayed eighteen years before. He kneeled by his bed in his room at the Tully Hill clinic and prayed, "Jesus! Save me, Jesus!" There was no blaze of light, no thrilling wave of electricity. The transformation in Scott, however, cannot be denied.

In the next weeks, Scott and Jean talked about nothing but God's will for their lives. Jean told Scott how to believe in Jesus. Scott told Jean how she needed to get straightened out with the Lord, too. It would be a struggle for them both, perhaps even a greater struggle for Jean, but they felt that Jesus was their only hope. They prayed together for the first time in their marriage. They began reading the Bible, and Scott was amazed, for the first time in his life, how the Book gave him courage, comfort, and direction.

Scott and Jean had a lot of re-building to do. They had to re-build their reputations. Their finances were in ruins, their house about to be foreclosed. Jean had to make the difficult first step back across the threshold of the church for their first meeting with the pastors. Hardest of all, they had to rebuild trust with their children and with each other. It was hardly a honeymoon, but we can gladly report that they have now succeeded on all points. The struggle was worth it.

It has been over twelve years since Scott and Jean took their last drink, puff, snort, pop, or shot for the sake of a buzz. Aside from what a doctor may have prescribed, the hardest drug Scott has taken would be the fireball candies he likes to suck on while he operates a crane.

Scott and Jean have since made themselves loved by all who know them and valuable assets in the body of Christ. Gentle, steady Scott has been a great help in ministering to the sick in the church, and together, Scott and Jean have aided numerous Sudanese refugees in resettling in Syracuse. Their great prayer is for more to do for Jesus.

Scott used his expertise as a heavy equipment operator to dig the foundations for the church's new building, but to him the most memorable part of the construction project was an installation that he didn't even help with. When he saw the new baptismal tank installed into a rough frame behind the pulpit, he cried the tears of thankfulness and joy. He remembered the day he was baptized and how the Holy Spirit filled him with love and power while he was in a similar tank. He thought of all the souls who would be dunked in this new tank in the future, their immersion in the water symbolizing the end of bondage to the sinful flesh. Others would have the same opportunity to be free. As it was for Scott, how true would be the Scripture for others: *If anyone is in Christ, he is a new creation; the old has gone, the new has come!*[*]

---

[*] 2 Corinthians 5:17.

# PART IV:  GOD'S WILL
## --Several Ways to Find God's Way

## CHAPTER ELEVEN

# The Worried Parents

*1 Samuel 23:12 Again David asked, "Will the citizens of Keilah surrender me and my men to Saul?"*
*And the LORD said, "They will."*

This is one of the interesting stories when the Lord said something would happen, but it didn't. Saul never arrived in Keilah even though the Lord said, *"He will,"* and the citizens of Keilah never turned David over to Saul even though the Lord said, *"They will."* Why? David left the city before either event could take place. The Lord revealed the future to David, so David could alter that future. Apparently, the Lord was not worried that he be forever recorded as making a prediction that was never fulfilled!

This case of the Lord being "wrong" in a prediction doesn't make us distrust the Lord at all. It's plain what was going on. The Lord was indeed certain about the future. To be more precise, however, he was certain about *one possible future.* If David stayed in Keilah, and if he trusted his security to the citizens of Keilah, he was certainly doomed. It was a way of warning David that he would have to skedaddle if he wanted to survive as a free man. The Lord was helping David.

In fact, David prayed to the Lord because he wanted help from the Lord to find the *best* future. David felt very vulnerable, so he sought for collaboration with the Lord. The Lord came through, helping David understand that his best future was certainly not in Keilah!

The existence for us of many futures may be a little troubling. It can make us feel unsettled, a little like our lives are a "Let's Make a Deal" game in which we have to take our chances with one of many doors. It may be a little scary to wonder just how much of our futures God is leaving for us to decide. It's a lot of responsibility that is very sobering. But we do not have to worry.

First, I am not saying anything new in a practical sense. Even if we may recite a religious creed that affirms God micro-manages every detail of the universe, all people who are mentally healthy down here at street level live with a deep appreciation of cause and effect. We look both ways before we cross the street. We pay our insurance premiums. We don't leave matches where the children can reach them. In other words, we don't simply throw caution to the wind because we trust that God has our futures in his hands.

We perfectly understand that if we make too many wrong choices, pain and/or loss is inevitable. We all know that if we put our trust in unfaithful people or erroneous ideas, we will get burnt. On the other hand, if we exercise wisdom in our decisions, we will have a better chance to prosper. All mentally healthy people accept conditions, contingencies, and probabilities, no matter what they recite during their religious education. We should probably realize that a creed that is not worth living is not worth memorizing and reciting.

Second, there is good news. The Lord has every intention of helping us find a better future if we will only consult him like David did. We might think that the Lord only said, *"They will,"* because it was the way to convince David to do what the Lord knew he would do from the start. The trouble is, this line of reasoning turns the Lord into a mere scriptwriter, a master of illusion, and us into his "Punch and Judy Show." I much prefer to think that the Lord honestly and plainly meant what he said, and that today, he still desires to work with us as he worked with David. The best news is that God speaks. It is up to us to listen.

Like David, Rob and Sherry believed that the Lord was telling them that their best future was not in a certain place. In their case, the place was a certain community in Florida where they had begun rearing their children. The warm Florida climate, owning their own house, and Rob's good job were not comforting them. Rob and Sherry were worried about their children's *spiritual* future, so they began to talk to the Lord about it.

Rob and Sherry already had two young boys. They were hoping to still try for a girl. Sherry, as a Christian from childhood, and Rob, as a Christian from his teen years, had married with every intention of rearing their children in Christ. That meant family devotions, Sunday school, church attendance, a daily emphasis on character building, and definitely a Christian school.

Rob and Sherry brought their young family to a number of churches around the area where they lived, but they were troubled by the spiritual condition of their surroundings. The lifestyle in their community was generally "fast"—fast to drugs, sex, and alcohol for the young. They were also scared by the sloppy brand of Christianity they saw around them, which seemed overly tolerant of a "fast" status quo in their community.

A crisis came when there was a scandal among the leaders of the Christian school to which they planned to send their children. The scandal renewed Rob and Sherry's prayer for a spiritually safe home in which to rear their children. They were even willing to consider relocating.

At the same time, Sherry's brother Bill had begun attending Living Word Church in faraway Syracuse. Both Rob and Sherry had grown up in Central New York, so they had some familiarity with the area. Any talk of Syracuse meant only two things to them: the average winter snowfall of about ten feet that blows off Lake Ontario and the biting cold that goes along with it. With an average 205 cloudy days per year, Syracuse was not sunny Florida. But Bill kept telling them about exciting things in "that church" up north.

Rob and Sherry were thinking about relocating, but they were assuming they would put in new roots someplace else in Florida. A return from the Sunshine State all the way to the Snow Capital of North America? Leave a decent job? What could possibly justify such a drastic step?

Sherry's brother Bill was an experienced Christian man and ex-minister. Bill reported that the church meetings in Syracuse had enthusiastic praise, prayer, and worship. The preachers proclaimed a strictly Biblical message. The pastor took tending and protecting the flock very seriously and tried to do his job diligently. There was a spirit of family togetherness among the members. Maybe most drawing of all, the church had its own school for children from pre-kindergarten through grade twelve.

Rob and Sherry knew they had to visit the church on their next family visit north. They had seen such a spiritual rejuvenation in Bill. They found out that a number of their nephews and nieces were coming to Christ as a result of the church in Syracuse. It was the kind of spiritual vibrancy that they wanted for their own family.

Bill was fuming about what happened when Rob and Sherry visited the church in Syracuse. The entire meeting was dedicated to Living Word Academy, the church's new school. The school was a relatively new endeavor for the church, and several parents, one after another, went to the pulpit to explain what the school meant to them. They each described the growth and happiness they saw in their children. The pastor then exhorted the congregation to get behind the project. He shared a number of verses from the Bible that encourage parents to diligently rear their children in the faith. Bill was upset because he had been praying that the Lord would powerfully and precisely direct Rob and Sherry to move north. He hoped for prophecies and special visitations by the Holy

Spirit. Instead he figured the church was throwing away a chance at impressing his sister and brother-in-law by devoting an entire service to such a mundane project. Rob and Sherry had to calm Bill by explaining that while the topic of the meeting might not seem to be an answer to his prayer, it was actually the perfect answer to theirs! It almost scared Rob and Sherry that the meeting was so perfect for them. Could the Almighty care so much for one little family?

Rob and Sherry could readily pick out any number of things that they didn't like in the church up north. The services weren't as predictable as they were used to. They were longer. The hand clapping, hand raising, and noisy worship felt awkward, even embarrassing. The pastor didn't strike them as particularly warm.

For that matter, even if all other objections failed, they could just shiver when they thought about the cold that was only about six or seven months away.

Even so, a thought kept nagging. What was in the future, ten or fifteen years ahead, for their children? Driving south to their Florida home, they each silently asked the Lord, like David did: "If we stay where we are in Florida will it hurt our children, Lord?"

Just south of Washington each felt the Lord's response, "It will."

Separately, and in their own minds each one asked the Lord, "Will the liberal churches in our community in Florida surrender our children over to confusion and disappointment?"

Each one felt the same response, "They will."

As the tires of their car hummed south on the pavement of I95, they turned to each other and spoke almost simultaneously, as if they were in the middle of a conversation: "We'll have to sell the house."

Arrangements did not go smoothly just because the Lord was leading them to this move. It surely was easy enough for Rob to end his job; as soon as he made it known he was moving north to New York, his company terminated him, no discussion necessary. Rob's search for another temporary job was fizzling out, seeing that he was only planning on being in the area for a short time. Sherry didn't have to quit a job because she was a stay-at-home mom. The next order of business was selling their home. It was a down year for real estate, and no offers were coming in. They were stuck with their mortgage and no income to help pay it.

Without a job, Rob was eerily free to relocate his family north and begin his job search in the Syracuse area. At least they could use the summer to settle in their new home and enroll their youngest boy in the Living Word Academy for the fall semester. But unless Rob found a job soon, their savings would not hold out, paying for regular living expenses plus moving, rent in Syracuse, a mortgage in Florida, and now tuition at the private Christian school. This was definitely the move of a lifetime.

In one way the first months back in Syracuse flew by—the monthly bills all came due sooner than they could believe, and the savings seemed to evaporate. In another way time was crawling. The days between job interviews or news of someone looking at the house down in Florida were nearly intolerable. Yet Rob and Sherry, with faith in the Lord's leading, did not waver about their decision. They were investing everything they had in a good future for their children.

The Lord is sometimes called the "God of 11:59." David might have called the Lord by this name when he was almost trapped in Keilah. The name means that the Lord seems to wait until the last minute to turn around our prospects. At least it seems that way when our faith is getting tested to its limits, and it was certainly true in Rob and Sherry's case. All the puzzle parts started coming together when they were literally down to their last few dollars.

Not only did Rob finally land a good job that he has kept for over twenty-five years, and not only did the house in Florida sell for a fair price. Rob and Sherry had another son and finally, their daughter. All four of their children graduated from Living Word Academy. They are together, they are happy, they have the peace and the wholesomeness they were reaching for. Two of their four children are married. They have their first grandchild who lives just a mile up the road. Rob and Sherry are sure the Lord led them to the better future.

## CHAPTER TWELVE

# The Swamp Runner

*Jonah 2:6 "To the roots of the mountains I sank down; the earth beneath barred me in forever. But you brought my life up from the pit, O LORD my God."*

The VeggieTales full-length animated movie got the main idea as well as any Bible commentary—the book of Jonah is the story of second chances. According to the word of the Lord proclaimed by the prophet Jonah, the utter destruction of the great Assyrian capital city Nineveh would commence in forty days because God's patience for their wickedness had dried up. According to the Bible, Nineveh was *"the city of blood, full of lies, full of plunder, never without victims."*[*] But destruction did not come after forty days because the Lord gave them another chance.

The forty-day countdown cut deep in one way and prodded in another. As a cutting condemnation, it meant that the Almighty had precisely fixed the time for the city's judgment. The exactness of the forty-day countdown implied an absolute future, an irresistible future. After all, if the word of the Lord was sincere when it pronounced this unquestionably precise future, who could rewrite the script? Forty days is forty days. Done is done.

---

[*] Nahum 3:1.

On the other hand, the prophecy begged a question. Why not destroy the city at the end of the first day if it was already judged as a whole to be guilty of a litany of capital offenses? It wasn't like the Lord was prone to waffling. In fact, he was in a rage over the city's sin. Yet the forty-day delay at least gave the city time in which to contemplate their corporate and individual sinfulness. What good could contemplation do?

The only reasonable purpose for giving them a countdown to destruction could be to goad the city into turning away from the wickedness that was taking them down. In other words, the Ninevites might hope that an unstated "Unless...," a *contingency*, lay hidden between the lines of Jonah's message. Might they do something to change God's mind? The city's king expressed their one chance: *"Who knows? God may yet relent and with compassion turn from his fierce anger so that we will not perish."** So the king ordered city-wide humiliation and repentance.

How right he was! For God suspended their sentence: *When God saw what they did and how they turned from their evil ways, he had compassion and did not bring upon them the destruction he had threatened.*† The future was not as unchangeable as the forty-day countdown had made it sound.

The Nineveh's reprieve leads us to an intriguing thought about God's omniscience. God knows people's destinies; for instance, he knew the city of Nineveh was going down in forty days. But those destinies seem also open to change. God's "knowledge" must not be simple knowledge. It's probably a kind of knowledge that is beyond us to comprehend. He apparently knows the roads of life we *might* choose, but the road we *will* choose appears, at least from our perspective, to be an open matter. C. S. Lewis, the famous British apologist whose statement introduces this book,

---

* Jonah 3:9.
† Jonah 3:10.

assesses the mater bluntly in his book *Mere Christianity*:
"Everyone who believes in God at all believes that He knows
what you and I are going to do tomorrow." But only a page
later Lewis concedes, "But it is not in the Bible or any of the
creeds."[*] In other words, while a theologian may, the Bible
will not, close the door on a chance to alter the future for good
or bad.

Even before the city of Nineveh received their second
chance, Jonah the prophet also got a second chance to obey
God. When the Lord first called Jonah to preach to Nineveh,
Jonah paid fare on a ship that would take him as far from God's
mission for his life as he could afford. He simply believed
(correctly!) the Lord might be merciful to Nineveh in spite of
his predictions of doom. In so doing, God would undercut
Jonah's credentials as a savant of unquestionable gifts. Jonah
fled because his credentials were more important to him than
the welfare of a great city, grotesquely so.

In response to Jonah's flight the Lord brought a storm
to the high seas. Jonah knew he was the one truly responsible
for the peril to all those aboard the ship with him, so he urged
the sailors to save themselves in the only way possible, by
tossing him over the rail. With the ship filling with seawater,
they finally yielded to his logic. A prayer-poem describes
Jonah's desperation after a huge fish gulped him down in a
single mouthful: *"I have been banished from your sight... The
engulfing waters threatened me, the deep surrounded me;
seaweed was wrapped around my head. To the roots of the
mountains I sank down; the earth beneath barred me in
forever."*[†] Jonah was certain, once he found himself swimming
in the gastric fluids of a great fish's belly, that his life was over,
and his relationship with the Lord was irredeemable.

It's hard for me to think that the story of Jonah is not
intended to be comical. Once Jonah was suitably humbled, the

---

[*] Lewis, 170-171.
[†] Jonah 2:4-6.

fish burped up the seaweed-entwined prophet onto a beach as so much driftwood. Wetter, probably a lot smellier, definitely surprised, but none the worse for wear, Jonah made good on his second chance to deliver his message of doom (and hope) to the wicked city. Nineveh must have looked a little silly, too, after they heard Jonah's message, for the repentant king ordered even the farm animals to be covered in sackcloth as an expression of the city's collective regret before God. Imagine every man, woman, child, and animal moping about town with a sackcloth prayer shawl draped over their heads!

Finally Jonah made himself absurd—sulking, griping, even wishing to die—not just because he observed God relent in his judgment of the great city. His shade vine was destroyed in the night by a worm sent by God. The Lord mocked him, *"You have been concerned about this vine, though you did not tend it or make it grow. It sprang up overnight and died overnight. But Nineveh has more than a hundred and twenty thousand people who cannot tell their right hand from their left, and many cattle as well. Should I not be concerned about that great city?"** It seems that even the Lord has a sense of humor.

At Living Word Church we have a brother in Christ who loves to entwine humor and the teaching of God's Word. Mike has an everlasting smile and an infectious laugh. Most importantly, he exudes joy when he shares the Word of God, always able to find the lighter side of a situation. Like both Jonah and Nineveh, Mike's life also testifies that the Lord is the God of second chances. Mike's first chance came when he turned to Christ as a nineteen year old.

Mike's conversion was dramatic, and indications were that he had every intention to turn his back on the drugs, booze, and crime that shamed him before God. He threw out his drug

---

* Jonah 4:10-11.

paraphernalia and destroyed his rock music collection. He discarded the uniform of his rebellion, the army jacket and dirty jeans; he cut his hair and shaved. He went to church every chance he got. Pushing drugs, bar fights, and jail time were the past. The dark side was dead.

The speed and degree of change in him was an awesome display of God's saving power, and Mike was so filled with the Lord he began to tell everyone he could about his conversion. It seemed as though the Lord had sovereignly snatched Mike from the mire of sinfulness just like the Lord said he would, *"I am found of them that sought me not."*[*] Unfortunately, however, he still had some growing up to do. Like the city of Nineveh and the prophet Jonah, Mike would soon need to pray from the depths of hopelessness to the God of second chances.

After six or seven months as a believer, the disciplines of the Christian life started getting boring to the high-energy nineteen year old. Some of Mike's old carousing buddies kept calling on the phone and luring him to "party on." Then some old girlfriends started advertising that they were available. Mike's commitment to Jesus deteriorated fast, and he decided to take a dive back into the wild side.

Mike was surprised when he forsook the Lord to find those phone calls had not been a good indication of his previous party partners' interest in him. Even his old friends wouldn't respect his bouncing from them to Jesus and back again. Cut loose from his earlier friends, Mike began to run with a rougher crowd than ever in his life. It was like he was on a mission to prove he was *sincerely bad*. High on pot, LSD, and booze, he would play the role of "advance man" for a gang of ruffians, leading the way into bars and drawing first-punches, so the ruffians would have an excuse to bust heads. Mike became an expert in finding a bar's tipping point, the point when all hell would break loose. Then he would dodge.

---

[*] Isaiah 65:1.

The inevitable disaster came on a night when Mike went to a clambake. Amid the wild drinking, he hit on other men's girlfriends, emboldened by dope, booze, and his fierce pals. He couldn't care less about the rage he was creating in his wake. But he assessed his defenses poorly. At the tipping point a crowd rushed him out of the building where the clambake was being held while also seeming to block his cohorts inside. The truth be told, Mike's buddies had just tossed him overboard.

Once alone, Mike realized that two or three angry boyfriends plus four or five of their supporters were about to jump him. Clumsy from drugs and drink, he ran for his car just ahead of them. He didn't have time to drive away, but he did have just enough time to reach above the visor of his car for his switchblade knife. Mike whirled about and caught the first attacker's arm with the knife. The attacker shouted to warn the others, but another crazed man would have none of it. As he pounced on Mike, Mike opened up his belly with a single sweep of the six-inch blade. So incensed he did not even realize he had been cut, the man knocked Mike to his back and pummeled his face. Moments later, drained of both blood and rage, the attacker just rolled to the side and laid panting and moaning.

The crowd that had gathered was in shock. Mike, lumbering to his feet over the wounded man, was a wild-eyed animal covered in his own and another man's blood, holding a bloody knife. No one challenged him. Now punch-drunk as well as high, he fled to the nearby swamp.

Mike knew well a corner of the Cicero Swamp. He and his drug buddies would maneuver past deep mud pits to a particular tree to get high and talk. Sometimes they would imagine what a good hideout from the law the swamp would make, almost 4000 acres of dense and forbidding swamp, a harbor for mosquitoes carrying eastern equine encephalitis and the only remaining home in the world of the eastern massasauga rattlesnake.

In the pitch black and in the frenzy of terror, Mike splashed and groped his way through the swamp to his tree, hoping to avoid the mud pits he knew could swallow him. He dove into some high grass as he saw the leaves of his familiar tree reflecting bleeps of red light from atop the police cars now pulling up five hundred yards away by the road.

Slimy, stinking, and bloody, covered with long wet grass—Mike had become Jonah gasping for life in the belly of his foolishness. But he wasn't surrendering yet. If he was praying, it was only that he could skip town somehow.

He heard policemen out by the road shouting, presumably to him. They fired some shotgun blasts into the air. What did that mean? Mike dug himself more deeply into the weeds. Before long he heard voices nearby and footsteps through the swamp. A search was on. Would they shoot? One officer passed by only ten feet away. Mike held his breath, his face half-buried in slime, the mosquitoes tormenting him. The only way the cops could find him was to step on him.

The search didn't last an hour, and Mike began to breathe easier, figuring his flight to the swamp was a sage decision.

At dawn he cautiously raised his swollen, bloody face out of the weeds. He was surprised to find himself alone with the mosquitoes. Crouching low and dodging from tree to bush, he slogged out of the swamp. He had some friends in a house a mile up the road; he was sure they would get him a car. As he expected, he spied police cruisers at the nearest house, so he went wide.

There were no police in his friends' driveway. He sneaked to their door, and sure enough they anxiously brought him in, scanning up and down the road to see if anyone was watching. Mike was just about to realize they were actually scanning because they hoped the police *were* watching! His friends let him in only to turn him in by calling the police from a phone in a back room. When the police arrived, guns drawn, they saw the injuries to his head and face. Mike rode to the hospital in handcuffs.

Mike's thoughts didn't turn to the Lord in the swamp because he was still cranked up for flight. He was not yet facing the final countdown like Nineveh or sucking in his last breath like Jonah in the depths of the sea. Once arrested, however, the impossibilities of his situation began to press in as the old escape routes closed one by one.

For instance, when he first got out on bail, he thought he would escape into the party life and keep a couple girlfriends. It wasn't happening because Mike had become too "hot," that is, too much the target of police attention, for most of his cohorts in crime. Besides, he had new doubts about the risk-and-dodge game that had become his life story. Mike understood the main rule of that game. You only play risk-and-dodge if you are *stupid brave*. He just didn't have the old dumb confidence any more. The well-worn road of dissipation and crime was blocked.

So Mike thought he would go in the opposite direction. He contacted an old police friend, who saw potential in Mike as a sixteen and seventeen year old and guided him through his first troubles with the law back then. The officer informed Mike there was nothing he could do. Bridge out.

Finally his lawyer informed him that they had no defense. Not a single one of his old cronies who were at the crime scene was claiming Mike had acted in self-defense. If only one friend would testify on his behalf he could cast doubt on the assault charges, and Mike would have a chance in trial. No one wanted to know him. If the D.A. decided to press for the maximum charge of first-degree assault he could get 7 to 15 years in a maximum-security state prison. Even the trial-road appeared a washout.

His money almost gone from paying a lawyer that couldn't do much for him, looking at a long jail sentence, Mike began to consider the path back to Jesus. The trouble was that the Jesus-path seemed hopeless, too, because Mike simply believed he was doomed to damnation.

Mike's foray back to the wild life tormented him because he realized how he had squandered the saving grace of Christ seven months prior. Now he was sorry he had been so outspoken on behalf of Christ to his circle of cohorts. He had played the fool. He knew he had hurt the church people, too, by forsaking the cause of Christ.

Mike was sure the Lord was done with him for turning his back on the cross of Jesus. He started to think of his abandonment of Jesus as the greatest sin of his life, an unforgivable sin. By then Jonah's words had become the perfect description of the distance between him and God: *I have been banished from your sight.*

There was also a practical hurdle making a return to Christ seem impossible. A long prison sentence was about to start. Even if Mike could somehow imagine that the Lord would take him back, he could never imagine succeeding as a Christian in prison. He had already endured several jail sentences, enough to understand the transformation that comes upon a man when he is caged. He knew what is trivial outside of jail, maybe a pack of cigarettes or a card game, becomes a cause for war inside it. In the jungle of a state penitentiary, how could a man of morals and faith and love survive? He would rather live as a rotten sinner than fail Jesus again.

While waiting for his trial, Mike got an idea. Before he was again incarcerated he would go back to church just to say good-bye to his Christian brothers and sisters. Maybe he would even say he was sorry to them. He didn't like that he had run out on them, and he wanted to make that right. He kept assuring himself he would *not* re-dedicate his life to Jesus. He would just say good-bye to the Lord's people.

On his way into the church service Mike only made small talk. People seemed surprised and happy to see him, but he didn't want to start making serious farewells until he got a better feel for exactly how welcome he really was. While he delayed a little longer, the singing began, and he stood with the rest of the congregation. For some reason his knuckles whitened as he gripped the pew in front of him, almost as if he was being chased.

The familiar piano and organ, the cheery singing and clapping melted his heart before the end of the third song. He admitted to himself why he was really there. He was so sorry to Jesus, so sorry he had disappointed him. But he needed help. He couldn't say it, but at least he felt it: "Rescue me, Jesus, I'm drowning!"

Mike didn't need to hear any preaching this time. He fixed his eyes on a target, the rail at the front of the church, and he started down the aisle for it. He grabbed the rail and dropped to his knees. But he didn't know what to say. He wanted to do the right thing, but he felt dead inside. He began to wonder if maybe this lonely run for the altar rail was really no different than his run for a familiar tree in the swamp.

Some of his Christian friends were beside him, their hands on his shoulders as they prayed for him. The pastor, Brother Bob, came over to him, the Bible open in one hand, the other hand pointing: "Do you see here, Mike? It says, *'If we confess our sins, he is faithful and just and will forgive us our sins.'* * Just confess, Brother Mike, and you are forgiven. Don't wrestle with it. And we forgive you, too, and we are so glad you are back." The pastor hugged him, and Mike finally started to pray. Even so, he just wasn't sure if heaven was hugging him, too.

If Mike would succeed in finding a new and bright future, he would need love. It began on his return to church when his friends received him and prayed with him. Then Brother Bob hugged him and welcomed him back with an encouraging verse. In the next weeks, Brother Bob even went to the judge in his case and offered to take custody of him. So did his parents. Struggling mightily with his guilt, Mike was

---

* 1 John 1:9.

inclined to agree with the judge's response to them all: "No, Mike must pay his debt to society."

A sister in Christ got Mike a job where she worked, so he could work during the few months of freedom until his sentencing. When his new boss Irving found out Mike would be going to prison, he ordered the manager to hold his job for him until he got out, whatever time it took. Irving even had Mike's manager speak to the judge on his behalf. Mike began to hope.

Eventually Mike accepted the D. A.'s offer. He pled guilty to a second-degree assault charge. A typical sentence would be 4 1/2 to 7 years, so he was shocked when the judge sentenced him to only a year and a half in a county lock-up. Now it seemed even the judge was trying to give him another chance. So many people wanted to salvage something from his wretched life story. He wondered, "Is the Lord really behind all of this?"

Mike's time in the prison was indeed an ordeal in the jungle of anger and fear, as he knew it would be, but the environment of a county jail was not as hostile as a state prison, and he remained determined to hang on to Christ from first to last. Some of the other convicts began to call him, "Rev" because he would constantly quote the Bible to them. He counted down the days until he would be eligible for parole, "…forty, thirty-nine, thirty-eight…"

Mike was out on parole after seventy days, and the hand of love still stretched out to him. Some friends from church picked him up from prison. They wouldn't have him feeling like a second-class citizen. His old boss Irving was good to his word and more. Not only was his job waiting for him. Irving paid him while he was in prison and held the money in escrow, like a paid vacation! Mike's parole officer, the toughest one in the county with the highest rate of re-arrest, was surprised. Mike really did have a job, and he really could pay his rent.

Even so, shadows of guilt still lurked behind Mike. He just knew that those weeks of sin after he had actually tasted of the goodness of Christ were inexcusable. He not only cut a man wide open; he had wounded a community, a church, and his family. Worst of all, he felt like he had stuck a knife in Jesus. Jesus bled for his sins long ago on a cross at a place called Skull Hill. He could not bleed again!

One day as Christmas approached, something happened that helped Mike fully accept the Lord's complete pardon. He still tears up when he tells the story.

His employer Irving came into the warehouse. Mike hardly knew the aged Jewish man at the time because Irving always remained in the background of the business. All his dealings with Mike for six months—hiring him in the first place, talking with the judge, saving money for him while he was in prison—had been performed through Mike's manager. This time Irving had something to say to him personally as he handed him a sealed white envelope: "Make sure you have a nice Christmas, Mike." That was all. The owner of the company left as quietly as he had entered.

Mike opened the envelope. His hand trembled as he fingered the contents. Strangely, he felt a wave of relief. An elderly Jewish businessman had just given him, an ex-convict, five hundred dollars with which to have a nice Christmas. Somehow that man's generous act gave him faith in the Lord's love for him, a love he would never doubt again. Mike's shoulders relaxed for the first time in a long time. The self-imposed guilt was finally off his back. It wasn't that Jesus had bled again; it was that the same blood that gave him his first chance with Christ was giving him a second chance, too. He would from thence forward fully embrace his second chance from the Lord.

It has been over thirty years since Mike got his second chance, and he has done well with it. He went on to work for Irving for nearly twenty years until his beloved boss died.

Irving accepted a pocket New Testament from Mike, which for years they would read and discuss together as they became friends. Mike also married and then reared two daughters in the house he owns. He is a well-known and well-respected salesman in the contractor's supply business. The best thing of all is that he is well on his way down the Lord's path for his life as a godly man who loves and teaches the Bible in word and deed.

## CHAPTER THIRTEEN

# In the Desert

*Numbers 14:11 The LORD said to Moses, "How long will these people treat me with contempt? How long will they refuse to believe in me, in spite of all the miraculous signs I have performed among them?"*

The art of waiting is an important topic in a book about being partners. Two people can only work together if each is willing to wait for the other from time to time. One partner may hesitate, make a mistake, or be by nature slower. The other partner will have to wait in order to keep the collaboration intact. Some tasks can only be performed by one person at a time. The other has to wait. A disagreement may take a little time to overcome. There will inevitably be a need for a "time out."

Would the art of waiting be equally important for a partnership between God and man? According to the Bible verse for this chapter, it sounds like God sometimes has to wait for his people. He must wait for us a lot more than we wait for him! And it sounds like he can get irritated in the process.

If God does truly wait for us or get irritated while waiting, it means that God is in some way reacting. Waiting, after all, is something we decide to do in response to a situation. The idea of the Lord reacting or responding to us probably seems like a natural enough idea, but put in another way, it becomes a little uncomfortable for some. Waiting means he is, in a sense, dependent us. This "dependence" is offensive to some people's ideas about God because to them a God who waits or reacts does not seem completely in control.

If God is really perfect, they say, he can in no way be moved by or be dependent on anything or anyone. In fact, the Greek philosopher Aristotle expressed his idea of the totally independent God as "the Unmoved Mover." In this line of thinking a God who waits or gets impatient sounds too human. God should always be in control, "micro-managing" the universe, always getting his way. But I can think of a few reasons why waiting is in perfect keeping with God's being God.

First, God as the Bible depicts him only waits when and if he wants to. If he wants to act unilaterally, without any adjustments to his initial plans, he certainly does so. For example, we now wait, with fearful anticipation, for God's sovereignly designed and independently scheduled script—the Apocalypse of the book of Revelation. It's the epitome of pre-destination. On the other hand, if he wants to do a little ad-libbing in our individual lives based on what we do, who are we to say he is not acting like God should? The point is that when God is dependent or independent is totally his decision. If so, it seems to me that the Lord is not *absolutely* dependent on us. Furthermore, when the Bible portrays the Lord waiting, I think we can marvel at the relationship or partnership he sovereignly seeks and maintains with his creation. Surely, if the Lord chooses to wait for us, we can't reasonably demand that he apologize for not being god-like enough.

Second, the ability to wait probably makes us like God rather than imagines his being like us. God made us in his image, the Bible says. The full significance of being made in the image of God is an open question. But one trait of himself that God certainly programmed into mankind is the capability for collaboration. It includes the abilities to communicate, share, and respond to each other. It also includes one ability that is critical for continuing collaboration—the ability to wait. Our capabilities to wait and collaborate are truly divine.

Third, a God who is totally and always independent and eternally serene is the construction of a "perfect" God that is handed down to us from the Greek philosopher Plato and generations of his followers. But Plato must not have influenced the writers of the Bible at all. Beside the fact that much of the Bible was written before Plato lived, a great deal of the Bible's portrayal of the Lord plainly fights against the Greek idea of "perfection." If the Bible stresses anything about the Lord, it's that he wants to collaborate with us. It's amazing, really. Not that it is so surprising that the Almighty wants to talk and wants us to listen. The amazing part is that he also chooses to take us seriously when we talk. Put another way, the God of the Bible is all-powerful, but he is also personable. He often responds to our prayer, and he sometimes waits until we pray before he will act on our behalf.

The Bible verse for this chapter is God's response when the children of Israel were first on the border of Canaan, the region God had promised to them for a national home. Prior to the Lord's frustration with them, they decided to send twelve scouts on a reconnaissance mission to determine the richness of the land and the strength of its inhabitants. All twelve scouts agreed the land was a delightful piece of real estate having formidable inhabitants in fortified cities. However, the scouts were divided about Israel's prospects for conquering the inhabitants.

Ten scouts thought conquering the land was a pipe dream and grieved that they had ever been so foolish as to imagine that they might acquire the beautiful land for themselves. They lamented at their own weakness compared to the people they would have to conquer: *"We seemed like grasshoppers..., and we looked the same to them."** Their discouraging report deflated the confidence of their young

---

* Numbers 13:33.

nation. Most of the children of Israel grumbled at having come so far across a desert only to be informed that their goal was the impossible dream.

However, two of the scouts, Joshua and Caleb, preferred to believe the Lord's promise in spite of Canaan's formidable inhabitants. Joshua and Caleb could not accept that the Lord would bring his chosen people to the verge of fulfilling his promise only to drive them into an immoveable barrier. Joshua and Caleb said of the Canaanite people, *"We will swallow them up. Their protection is gone, but the LORD is with us."* [*]

So the people were divided, most following the cynical scouts, a few siding with Joshua and Caleb. The cynicism actually marked the tenth time the majority of Israel doubted the Lord as a nation, so it should be no wonder that the Lord became impatient with this national malady of defeatism.

As a result of the delay, he replaced the promise of immediate victory with a new and terrible promise: the Lord would make Israel wander in the desert for forty years until the doubting generation died off. The Lord would take good care of his people during their wandering, but they would absolutely not, as a nation, enter the Promised Land until forty years had elapsed and the cynical generation had expired. They made the Lord wait; now the entire nation would have to wait. Even faithful Joshua and Caleb would have to wait. At least the Lord gave Joshua and Caleb a special promise, that they would survive the ordeal and accompany their nation into Canaan.

One more detail of the story shows how fragile a partnership with the Lord can be. When the children of Israel heard how irritated the Lord was, they felt, en masse, regret that they had doubted him those ten times. They confessed their sin and decided to make it right by immediately charging into the Promised Land. They attempted to exude confidence. "God's people are in the house!" they thought. Only when

---

[*] Numbers 14:9.

they charged ahead, the Lord wasn't working with them, and the inhabitants of the land squashed the invasion force like so many bugs. Israel retreated from the Promised Land on grasshopper legs. They had missed their opportunity. Now they had to wait, as the Lord said.

The case is an intriguing example of how the will of the Lord can be a moving target. At first the target was for the children of Israel to conquer the Promised Land right away. When the people doubted the Lord, he became angry and his will for the children of Israel changed. He insisted they wander in the wilderness for forty years before he would help them conquer the Promised Land. The new target for the children of Israel was to trust the Lord to provide for them while they wandered in the desert.

Two of my friends also had a test in the desert during which they learned to trust the Lord together. In fact, their test was on some of the very same dust of the Arabian Peninsula where the children of Israel had to wander. Thankfully, Barb and Lou's experience in Saudi Arabia didn't have to last forty years.

Barb and Lou had a good marriage and two young children. They enjoyed each other and were excited about the prospect of rearing a family. Lou had managed to secure a job with a prominent company in Syracuse, so they had a new house with "the stuffings"—new furniture, all the gadgets and toys a young mother and her children could want. Barb and Lou enjoyed planning their future together. They didn't argue. They were partners. Until, that is, they began to go their separate ways.

Lou was becoming two men in one package. One was the first Lou—responsible, fun, and communicative. The newer Lou was the hard-charging businessman. The businessman Lou loved competing in an international arena, and as he succeeded, receiving better assignments, greater responsibility, and a higher salary. The cost of success was the time his wife and children would have to do without him.

In the meantime, Barb became a different woman. She was truly proud of her rising business star husband, but she also felt a hollow in her own bosom that husband, children, house, and furniture could not fill. Searching, she read the testimony of a criminal who turned to Christ, talked with a Christian friend, and did some long, hard thinking. In the sixth year of their marriage, at age twenty-seven, she knelt bedside one night when Lou was out of town on business, and asked Jesus to forgive her of her sins and take the reins of her life. She began attending church once, twice, and sometimes more every week. She finally found a church home at Living Word Church. This was working. She had sought for help and peace, and she found both in Jesus.

For the next five years Lou would come to church a few times a year, but he always refused to match Barb's interest in serving the Lord. He first figured his wife was going through the "born-again stage" of life, which would soon pass. When sufficient time passed to force a dismissal of the fad notion, Lou's pride set in. Whenever he visited Barb's church or was around her church friends, he resented that he felt like a marked man. He didn't appreciate some religious fanatics counting the conversion of his soul as a spiritual trophy.

When Barb first came to Christ, Lou was just beginning the steepest part of his ascent in his business career. As he climbed the rungs of success, Barb saw less and less of her husband. He started traveling overseas for four to six weeks at a time, only a month or two at the home office between trips. Lou racked up visits to Ireland, France, Vietnam, Dubai, Nicaragua, Panama, New Zealand, Australia, and over fifty other countries on every continent except Antarctica.

There was a weird disconnect. When he was away, Barb's partner would never call or write. Never. Ever. He was too pre-occupied; there was no room in his mind for anything, neither wife nor children, except running the foreign factories his company assigned him to manage. Since it was before cell phones or e-mail became common, Barb often didn't even know where Lou was or how to contact him. After a while, even when Lou was in Syracuse, business began demanding that he often get home late because he was schmoozing a client or strategizing about a new project. The whiskey on Lou's breath when he did come home started making Barb dizzy with worry.

Would Lou run the car into a bridge abutment some night and kill himself? Were there seductive women at these "business" sessions? Overseas, Lou sometimes went to third world countries against the advice of the US State Department travel bulletins. Would Lou be thrown in some dungeon to rot forever? Might someone kidnap him to coax a large ransom from his rich American company? Lou's long communications blackouts made pretty rich psychological soil for germinating some horrifying nightmares.

Her Christianity notwithstanding, Barb sometimes wondered if she still liked the man she was married to. She surely hadn't married with the idea of having only half a husband. Fortunately, one verse from the Bible, so direct and specific about her dilemma, clinched her resolution to honor her marriage commitment: *And if a woman has a husband who is not a believer and he is willing to live with her, she must not divorce him.*[*] In other words, even when Barb wasn't sure if she liked her husband, she *knew* the right thing to do was to remain faithful to him.

Barb avoided the common mistake many believers make when they turn to Christ but their spouses resist. Whatever she might imagine was going on during Lou's long absences, she would not imagine that her marriage had not been God's will in the first place. She wasn't taking her own salvation as an opportunity to call her marriage a foolish, pre-

---

[*] 1 Corinthians 7:13.

Christ choice that needed undoing. On the contrary, like most married people, Barb and Lou made their vows before witnesses, a licensed clergyman, and the presence of God. God used the institution of marriage to unite them, and as Jesus said, *What God has joined together, let man not separate.*[*] Barb knew God's will for her was to wait and pray and endure. Still, Lou seemed clueless as to what God's will was for him.

Just as the children of Israel were delayed forty years before entering the Promised Land because of their unbelief, Barb would not experience God's intention to give her a whole husband and a whole family for five years plus. Barb and Lou were, in a sense, as divided from each other as faithful Joshua and Caleb were from their ten cynical colleagues.

Barb usually played it smart as she waited for Lou to come to Christ. She wouldn't pressure him to come to church. She would do her best to leave him a good breakfast on Sunday mornings, so he would have no reason to grumble at her absence. If she went to church on a weeknight, she would bathe the children first and get them in their pajamas. She didn't scold the "business Lou" for being distracted. No tantrums. No manipulations. She mostly cheerfully trusted that the Lord could and would speak to Lou better than she ever could.

Barb admits losing her patience one time about a red Buddha statue on their fireplace mantle. Lou brought the little fat man home from a business trip, and as a Christian she hated it. Fed up one day, she put it in a bag, dropped it on the garage floor, and threw the broken statue in the garbage. She later told Lou what happened, conveniently leaving out the one detail. She had dropped it on purpose.

Lou remembers one night when a conversation did indeed wax desperate. Maybe he noticed sternness in Barb's demeanor, or maybe she seemed to be trying too hard at being nice. When he pressed her, Barb asked for a heart-to-heart.

---

[*] Matthew 19:6.

Lou knew a confrontation was coming. She expressed her dissatisfaction with this unknown intruder into their marriage who went traipsing all over the world on business. His name was Lou, but he wasn't the man Barb married.

The businessman took the offense: "Stand up, Barb." She was put back on her heels by the physical nature of the command, a little scared at his vehement demeanor. "Turn around. Look at all this, Barb. The house, the kids, the furniture—this is all me, you know. I couldn't give you all this if I didn't do what I do."

Barb replied quietly, but her eyes were fixed on Lou's, "I don't want stuff. I want you." As a good businessman Lou knew when it was time to listen hard. Barb was not a "high maintenance" wife. She never asked for anything. This talk was an unusual glimpse into Barb at her core. He respected his wife, her sense of fairness, and her honesty, so her words struck Lou to the core. Their talk that day started him reassessing to whom or what he belonged. He wanted to be whole for his wife, his children, and himself. Lou wasn't going to turn to Jesus for some time, but this was a conversation that stuck with him.

During the Sunday morning church service when Lou finally surrendered to Christ, half of him—the husband-and-family-man half—stared forlornly, deflated and excluded from the spiritual interests of his dear wife. The businessman half couldn't wait for the service to end. Then a man Lou knew for years, a plumber by trade, approached Lou where he sat in church. The plumber offered to accompany Lou to the special habitation of all pipe-jockeys: "Look, Lou, you don't have to walk down that aisle in front of all these people to turn to Jesus. How about if you and I head quietly back to the bathroom? We can pray there. No one needs to know what you're doing."

The knot in Lou's stomach came undone. The plumber's invitation came as a revelation: this guy was trying to think of a way to make it easier for him because the objective of Barb's believing friends, he suddenly realized, was not to make a spectacle of him. The quest for his soul was not a competition, like a sale. He had not been willing to admit that his elusiveness had more to do with his own pride than some twisted motivations in Barb's brothers and sisters in Christ.

When Lou sidestepped to the end of his row of chairs, the plumber in tow, he didn't turn left to go to the bathroom at the back of the auditorium. He wasn't heading for the exit either. He turned right to pray at the front of the auditorium. Lou always said, "If you're going to do something, you might as well do it right."

Barb had been seated a few seats away from Lou, some relatives between them, and her eyes were closed in prayer at the moment Lou headed to the aisle. Someone tapped her on the shoulder. "Barb, Lou just went forward to pray." First Barb couldn't believe her ears; then she couldn't believe her eyes. There was Lou, kneeling in prayer at the front of the church. By this time the entire congregation started clapping and shouting praises to God as if a blind man had just received his sight.

Barb didn't know exactly how to interpret Lou's walk down the aisle. She certainly didn't sense that Lou or their marriage had reached some final destination. She sensed it was more like the first leg of long journey. She couldn't have been more right because Jesus would make Lou whole by bits and pieces over a long period of time.

Phase one of Barb and Lou's journey was Lou's walk the length of the church auditorium. Phase two began with a long plane ride to the Arabian Desert, site of the Israel's forty years of wandering in the desert wilderness. In fact, Barb calls her two years in Saudi Arabia her personal "wilderness experience" because she learned there the same lesson the children of Israel learned, to trust completely in the Lord while she waited.

Lou took on this company assignment in Saudi Arabia within months of his commitment to Christ, so we can hardly say his business drive died with his commitment to Jesus. The assignment required a long-term placement, and Lou had an opportunity to relocate his family there for the duration. He not only took the opportunity for the career and financial gains it would give him. To his credit, he believed the trip was a gift from the Lord during which he could get alone with his family away from the distractions of booze and business in the hyper-competitive American marketplace. He would come home every night to their double-wide trailer on an American compound in the middle of a desert. They would have neither TV nor phone. As it turned out, in spite of Lou's golden motivations, the expedition turned out to be a pretty lonely time of waiting for Barb.

When Barb boarded the TWA 747 jumbo jet to join Lou in Saudi Arabia she wasn't nearly as revved up as her children by the novelties of eating dinner and watching a movie while flying. She was preoccupied with the headline news of earlier that day: Iranian Militants Storm US Embassy, Take Forty-four Americans Hostage. The events in Tehran would make entire Middle East more dangerous. It was an ominous sign that put frowns on a lot of her friends and family as they waved good-bye.

A happier sign, albeit of a much humbler size, came next. Barb packed a Bible in every piece of their luggage because Bibles weren't allowed in the fundamentalist Muslim nation. She figured at least one Bible might escape all the inspectors' prying eyes. Maybe Lou's advice on ways to hide them between ladies' underwear worked because not one Bible was confiscated.

This same kind of contrariety of troubling developments versus spiritual support continued throughout Barb's venture in Saudi Arabia. To the bad: Barb arrived to find many of the other wives of American businessmen were heading home because the Middle East had become so volatile.

To the good: Barb and Lou found American missionaries on their compound. To the bad: they were warned that travel into the cities could be dangerous. To the good: poor non-nationals who were in Saudi for the factory jobs joined them in their home on the compound for rousing prayer and worship services.

To the bad: One day while Barb was enjoying the pool on their compound a frantic neighbor ran to her. A car had backed over Barb's son, who was just learning how to pilot a new bike. The car's rear tire backed over her son's mid-section, the bike in a tangled mess beneath him. Fortunately, a neighbor shouted the car to a halt before a second tire could double the damage. Lou was impossible to reach. Alone in the emergency, Barb began to pray. To the good: A passerby brought Barb and her son to an infirmary nearby where a doctor gave her son first aid for some ugly abrasions. An ambulance finally arrived to take her son to the hospital where the injured boy was able to pass for a Saudi national because of his naturally dark skin. Doctors determined the boy's only injuries were the abrasions and some bruises on his arms. Barb and Lou believe the Lord had answered Barb's prayer for a miracle.

Then there were some everyday things. Something as seemingly benign as dust could become grievous; the never-ending chore of cleaning the yellow desert dust, wind-driven and finer than flour, drove Barb crazy. But good comfort for her mind came in the mail. Brothers and sisters in Christ back in Syracuse, many of whom Barb and Lou barely knew, sent letters and packages. One woman wrote Barb every week for the entire two years. Before Barb and Lou's expedition in the desert wilderness, Barb knew her pen pal only casually. The letters were like bread from heaven.

One day Lou didn't come home as expected. Midnight came, and still no Lou. Barb had no idea where he was, and they had no phone. She certainly couldn't drive to the city to look for him because women weren't allowed to drive. Her mind was tortured with a score of nightmarish guesses as to his whereabouts, but she had little she could do but calm herself with faith. She knew she and her husband were in the hand of the Lord no matter what dangers lurked.

The next day Lou walked in the door at midday. He explained that he had not closed his office the previous day for the Muslim time of prayer. For the violation he was arrested and spent the night in jail. The good part was that Lou came home as soon as possible to console his wife. To comfort her, he took the rest of the day off.

The multitude of bad-then-good's taught Barb that however bad things were, the Lord's provision was on the way. In other words, she not only learned to wait. She learned to trust the Lord while she waited. Trusting while she waited enabled her to wait with expectation of a turnabout. Trust calmed her and gave her good cheer.

Barb and Lou's expedition to the Arabian Peninsula ended, but the Lord's intention to make Lou whole still wasn't finished. We might say Lou was keeping the Lord waiting, but the Lord was patient and worked while he waited. It meant Barb had to wait, too, but she was more than willing. To her the change in Lou was cause for awe.

Home from Saudi Arabia, Lou was baptized as a public confession of his decision to live for Jesus. For the occasion he wore a three-piece suit into the baptismal. (Remember his motto about doing things right?) He started to find places of service in the body of Christ, for instance, by using his expertise in travelling to help the students at Living Word Academy to have memorable field trips. As the months fell from the calendar, Lou started *wanting* to go to church rather than only feeling like he *had* to go to church. He learned to give tithes, a tenth of his income, no hesitation, for the Lord's work. Alcohol fell by the wayside. Quitting smoking was especially hard for Lou, but he truly believed it was for the good of everyone he loved, so with the help of God's Spirit he even managed that. Each step for Lou was like another step into the Promised Land for his and Barb's marriage.

After some years, Lou's company wanted to send him on another assignment overseas, and he refused. Lou knew the refusal was corporate suicide, but by then his priorities had truly changed, and he was willing to let his refusal play out as it might. When the company then required him to pack up his family and take a position in Texas, he informed them that he couldn't merely be a company man any more. He was a family man first, and moving wasn't in the best interest of his family. He was part of a team in a local church, and moving wasn't in the best interest of his friends. If that was his position, his bosses informed him, they no longer had work for a man with his expertise in Syracuse. The company was letting him go. Lou felt so good when he left work that day. He knew where he belonged. He was whole.

For Barb it took five years of waiting after her own conversion for Lou to turn to Jesus, two more in the Arabian desert while they learned to trust the Lord together, and a couple more tacked on for good measure while Lou finally let go of that driving, competitive business life that so interfered with his God-given role as a family man. It was a long wait, but waiting is part of any partnership. The Lord himself was willing to wait. Why wouldn't Barb?

Now Lou calls Barb his "best buddy." He credits his present satisfaction in Christ to this perfect lady's patience and perseverance until he finally became whole. Now Lou's great desire is to leave to his children and the church a legacy of faithfulness to Jesus. He says, "You can't put a dollar sign on that."

Barb admits it took quite some time and a lot of adjustments while her partner lagged, but she also knows her marriage has finally entered their own Promised Land of sorts. This year they celebrated their thirty-ninth anniversary. And Barb is now positive she *likes* her husband.

## CHAPTER FOURTEEN

# The Forsaken Woman

*Acts 27:21-22 After the men had gone a long time
without food, Paul stood up before them and said:
"Men, you should have taken my advice not to sail
from Crete; then you would have spared yourselves
this damage and loss. But now I urge you to keep
up your courage, because not one of you will be
lost; only the ship will be destroyed."*

Is the Lord directly involved with every detail of our
lives? Not according to the Apostle Paul's storm-tossed
voyage and the shipwreck of Acts 27. As we shall see,
however, the Lord can providentially intervene to achieve
marvelous results even when people refuse to do his will.

I have often marveled at the place of Paul's shipwreck
in the list of difficulties he faced during his career. Paul bore
marks on his body inflicted at least ten times by persecutors
who sentenced him to prison, beat, whipped, flogged, and
stoned him. These sufferings make a certain kind of sense
because they were all the angry responses of those who hated
his preaching. Jesus warned his servants to expect
disagreement and sometimes even vehement hatred. Paul, in
particular, was a fiery proclaimer of teachings that represented
a radical departure from standard religions of his day. Some
people were bound to get angry.

But a storm and a shipwreck? Actually, Paul tells of
being shipwrecked not only once during his mission

labors, but three times. They are not in the same class of troubles as persecution. Weather and traveling graces might seem like they should be something for which the Lord would pick up the tab, especially on behalf of a handpicked servant. Couldn't the Lord have nudged these terrible storms aside with the strength of his mighty little finger? Couldn't the Lord have protected his servant, the great apostle, and helped his servant along on his mission to spread the Gospel by re-directing the winds? Not only did the Lord not intervene to change a typical weather pattern. Apostle Paul did not expect him to.

Paul said, *"Men, you should have taken my advice not to sail from Crete; then you would have spared yourselves this loss."* In other words, the loss was not necessary, as far as Paul was concerned. The loss was not God's will. It was a result of a bad choice to ignore the probabilities. Specifically, the Mediterranean Sea, on which they were sailing, was and is notorious for its rough seas in the winter. This weather pattern was common knowledge in Paul's day, so he recommended that the ship not risk a run into the open sea. The captain endangered all their lives by making the rash attempt to beat the odds.

Yet, Paul was also sure that they could stop even more loss if they would stick together, the result of a promise from none other than an angel: *"Do not be afraid, Paul. You must stand trial before Caesar; and God has graciously given you the lives of all who sail with you."*[*]

In spite of an angel's promise and Paul's subsequent pronouncement that everyone on board would survive, two weeks later, the situation became dire as the ship seemed to be approaching a rocky coast. Because the ship would likely crash into the rocks and kill all on board, the professional sailing crew planned a trick. (They cared little for Paul's word of angelic assurances!) They would pretend to service the ship's anchor, while in reality they were going to steal away on

---

[*] Acts 27:24.

the ship's one small lifeboat to save themselves. The passengers could fend for themselves.

Paul caught on to the ruse and revealed the plan to the military men on board the ship. He joined his revelation with some advice: *"Unless these men stay with the ship, you cannot be saved."** Paul may not have been worrying for himself. He had a divine promise that he would preach the Gospel in Rome, but he believed that the survival of the other people on board was contingent on sticking together.

The advantage of staying together made sense. The experienced sailors would be needed to pilot the ship as close to shore as possible before everyone would be forced to go overboard and swim the rest of the way to shore. Paul was sure that lives would be lost if the sailors would be allowed to abandon ship prematurely. He did not simply trust in the angel's promise that everyone would survive. In other words, Paul believed that obtaining their promise from the Lord depended on the use of good sense and teamwork.

This time the soldiers listened to Paul's advice and cut loose the small boat before the sailors could take it away. The soldiers realized with Paul that the sailors were more important to their survival than one lifeboat. In the end, everyone on the floundering ship did indeed swim safely to shore because the professional sailors managed to steer the floundering ship close to shore by the mouth of a creek. The Lord even did some miracles through Paul on the island of Malta where a wonderful story unfolded.

Let's consider the events as two plans, "Plan A" and "Plan B," both of which were equally God's will. Plan A was to stay in the harbor for the winter and wait for the gentle seas of springtime. Paul says that if they had followed God's Plan A, *"...you would have spared yourselves this loss."* But they didn't listen, they could no longer get back to port, and they had to sacrifice the cargo on the ship to even have a chance to

---

* Acts 27:31.

save their skins. In other words, the chance to do Plan A was lost forever once they were in the middle of the stormy sea. God's Plan B was the angel's promise. Plan B was to stick together and ride out the storm, so every life could be saved. Interestingly, if the professional sailors were allowed to depart prematurely, Paul believed that even Plan B would be scuttled.

Plan A and Plan B are not "the perfect will of God" and "the permissive will of God." Some Christians say that God has a precise set of steps that he has planned for our lives called the "perfect will of God." But he will also tolerate a little sloppiness on our part. They say we can live out God's "permissive will" when we don't choose exactly as the Lord wants us to. No doubt, the Lord is patient.

But Paul's ordeal at sea is not about sloppiness. It shows that God is gracious enough to still lead us even after an opportunity to execute his original plan is completely and permanently lost. We simply cannot turn back the clock or reverse the winds. Thankfully, even though a particular chance to serve the Lord in some specific way can be lost forever, that doesn't mean God's grace is lost forever. He will try again to lead us in another way. Again thankfully, the Lord doesn't respond to us, "You are not listening to Me! I'm done with you!"


The experience of a faithful Christian woman might help us appreciate the precious possibilities in God's "Plans B." For close to thirty years, Janis, a registered nurse who spent her nursing career in the Intensive Care Unit, has served the church in a multitude of ways. One particular ministry is a family affair for her. And maybe it's fitting that the ministry is in teaching people to swim safely—just in case the children of the church may find themselves in a shipwreck someday.

Each summer, Janis' husband and two lovely daughters join her in keeping scores of swimmers safe and helping to teach scores of children to swim at the beachfront of our church camp. Her husband, a professional engineer, designed and built the swimming dock at the beach. He, Janis, and often their daughters install the dock in the spring and remove it in the fall. Janis' two daughters have also served as lifeguards and swimming instructors with their mom. This effective marriage and family team is actually the result of Janis' second marriage, and this ministry is part of God's productive "Plan B" for her.

Any married couple, as they embark on life's journey, can be assured that the trials of life will sometimes toss the boat with wicked winds on hostile waves. It's very important for a couple to stick together and use good sense rather than to jump ship. They have vowed before witnesses, the state, and God himself that they will remain together through better and worse until death parts them. That's the Lord's Plan A for a marriage. God hates divorce. Jumping ship is intolerable to Jesus except for very special cases, which we won't explore here.

Janis knew and embraced God's expectations for her first marriage. She and her first husband were Christians when they married. Janis was certain of God's desire for them to make a life-long commitment. They had prayed again and again over their relationship. She certainly had no intention of failing, but to her dismay, her first marriage was on the rocks.

Her first husband hated the limits marriage put on him. It's a kind of rebelliousness that happens to a lot of men early in their marriages when they realize what a blow marriage will be to their independence. These guys just have to smarten up to realize how much better off they are with their brides!

In the case of Janis' first husband, the rebellion grew extreme. It was actually as much a rebellion against Christ as it was against the limitations that come with marriage. Janis first noticed that she was going to church alone more and more frequently. Then her husband began to substitute barhopping for church attendance. Once her husband emptied his pockets and illegal pills scattered over the floor. Janis began to find stashes of pot in this drawer or that, which she would flush down the toilet. It was becoming clear that her marriage, too, was also going down the tubes. The more Janis tried to reason with her husband the more an angry tempest raged in their home.

Then came the crusher. Her husband was running with other women. Janis' steadiness, wholesomeness, and volunteerism were not beautiful to him any more. In his evil self-love, he came to hate her and all that she stood for. After a little more than a year of marriage Janis' first husband moved out for a life of carousing, substance abuse, and unemployment. A year later they were divorced. Astonishing as it may sound, he wound up leaving the country to fly hot air balloons in Kenya. Janis could do little during her ordeal than watch God's Plan A for her life literally drifting away forever.

The loss was emotionally devastating. For Janis in particular, the emotional tearing from the man she loved was only part of her ordeal. She also felt like she was part of a scandal. Her life had become exactly the opposite of the wholesome example of love and faithfulness she believed the Lord wanted for her and her husband. She was ashamed to inform her family of her husband's departure because she felt she was letting them down. She feared, at the age of twenty-four, that she would forever be stigmatized.

The depression Janis felt was deep. She considered getting wasted in a lonely alcohol binge. But that didn't make sense because in the morning she would not only still be forsaken; she would be hung over. Speeding along the highway she considered a violent turn off the steepest embankment. She would die. It would be over. That didn't make sense either because she might do half a job. Then she would wind up like so many of the paralytics she cared for in the ICU. She chose instead three days of hiking and praying in a state park.

The Lord's will was lost. The wounds of disappointed love were raw. Perhaps even more agonizing was where her divorce put her. She was standing in the west when she thought she had headed east. The strongest resolution of her life was for her life story to herald the goodness of God. Now it seemed her life proclaimed the victory of darkness. Yet the Lord was not finished with his daughter. Janis only had to win the battle to believe the Lord, in his providence, had another plan.

Had she stepped out of the will of God for her life? She didn't know at first. The one thing she resolved was that until she found her answer, she would be every bit as faithful to the Lord as she had hoped her husband would have been to her. Thankfully, she realized in time. She had not stepped out of the Lord's will. Her husband had. The will of the Lord required collaboration.

The man that would one day become her second husband and the father of her daughters was watching the whole time. He admired and respected Janis for making the right choices during what he believed must have been the hardest ordeal of her life. In time, he thought, he would approach her.

We know the end of the story. Janis today feels like she has been restored. She can so courageously share her story here out of her deep thankfulness to the Lord.

As a pastor, I cannot go on record to encourage a single divorce and/or endorse a re-marriage. Because the details of every situation are so different, I don't feel like I can formulate the rules by which to decide for or against so many different cases. If so many cases are beyond me to decide, I don't feel I have any business making public pronouncements about any of them. Additionally, the facts and faults in a failing marriage relationship are practically impossible to discover fairly and objectively. Even the very search for the truth can devastate families, give long-lasting wounds to innocent people, and even split the church. A pastor is not a trial judge.

On the other hand, neither is he to be a rubber stamp. As a result, if the people in the church I pastor feel like they have to get divorced and/or re-married, they have to do it without me. It's a decision between them and the Lord. I will try to help them in Christ when the dust settles. We gladly serve a lot of divorced and re-married people.

All this said, I have no question that Janis and her second husband and the two daughters born to them are today in the very hand of the Lord. Their lives proclaim the bounty and grace of Christ, and the church thankfully enjoys their fellowship and receives their service.

The lesson shared by Paul's shipwreck and Janis' failed marriage? Someone may do the dumb thing, even the terribly painful and destructive thing, so that a particular opportunity to do the will of the Lord is lost forever. The Lord's intention for us may be wasted and impossible to retrieve. The Lord in his mercy and care may then provide us another possibility. It's a way to minimize our losses and live out "another will of God for our lives." We never want to miss out on the Lord's "Plan A," but if we do, he may guide us into his wonderful and productive "Plan B."

NOT EVEN GOD

# PART V: YOUR STORY

## CHAPTER FIFTEEN

# At the Brink

*Luke 13:4 "Those eighteen who died when the tower in Siloam fell on them—do you think they were more guilty than all the others living in Jerusalem?"*

Here Jesus refers to a disaster, about which very little is known today, but must have put the entire region in a buzz of speculation. If people in the Bible days were as inclined to stir up controversy as they are today, the fall of a great tower surely kindled arguments over why the tower was allowed to deteriorate into such disrepair, or why a large number of people were allowed to congregate under a menace. There would have been a hot search for someone to blame. When people began buzzing that the eighteen people who died were meeting with some sort of heaven-sent justice, Jesus felt compelled to weigh in: *"I tell you, no!"*[*]

We might compare the disaster at the tower of Siloam to the 1987 collapse of the Schoharie Creek Bridge a few miles east of Syracuse on the New York State Thruway. Heavy spring rains combined with snow melt to produce a once-in-fifty-year flood in the Schoharie Creek gorge.

---

[*] Luke 13:5.

The bridge carrying the cross-state superhighway over the gorge, being only thirty-something years old, was facing the greatest test in its lifetime. The fast and voluminous waters undercut the soils supporting pier number three of the bridge, and when the pier rolled into the resulting hole, a first span of over a hundred feet in length collapsed into the gorge below. A car and an eighteen-wheeler were on the span at the time. Before frantic motorists were able to wave to a stop all other traffic, three more vehicles drove off the broken edge into the eighty-foot abyss. In all, ten people died. The miles-long backup of traffic seemed like such a headache to motorists that morning until they learned the reason for it. Then they likely shuddered to envision their own freefall had they managed a three or five or ten minute earlier start to their day.

Imagine the exclamations of the first motorist that parked at the brink, the first in a long jam of people who survived their drives to work: "Oh, my God! The Lord spared me!" It's the expected kind of thing to say.

How appropriate would seem the Bible verse, This *is the day the LORD has made; let us rejoice and be glad in it!**  We might even say now, "Thank the Lord more people didn't die that day!" We *should* be glad more people didn't die; it could so easily have been worse. But can we get our arms around all our "harmless" thanksgiving really says?

"The Lord spared me!" also says—and means, even if we don't think of it like this—the Lord had something against the ten who died in the gorge. He didn't spare them. The claim implies God did not favor the dead as he had favored the survivors. Jesus would say, *"I tell you, no!"* The dead were no guiltier than the living. The living were no more favored than the dead.

It's the same problem faced by a soldier who survives a firefight while the buddies to his right and left are killed: "Why did God spare me? Why didn't he spare them?" Again,

---

* Psalm 118:24.

Jesus would tell us the thinking is wrong. Not only are we looking for answers in the wrong direction. We are even asking the wrong questions.

We are likely to accept that God did not end the lives of soldiers who die in battle or the ten people who die in a river gorge because we don't want to imagine the Lord plotting against them. We may be slower to accept the other side of the coin. Is it fair to say he *saved* all those people caught in a massive backup on the highway, those who at first damned an inconvenient delay because they didn't yet understand the cause of it?

Let's return for another pass by the ancient ruins of a disaster. Jesus denied any speculation that the Siloam Tower's fall was God-sent judgment. In so doing, he also meant to deny that surviving the disaster, no matter how close of a brush with death it may have been, was the result of some special favor of God. He is telling us to sever any connections between the tower collapse and the will of God. He literally accepted that the eighteen deaths were an accident. Those who died died by chance. That means, those who survived, survived by chance. Sure enough, an after-the-fact investigation of the tower by Jerusalem's engineers could produce explanations, responsibilities, and accountabilities almost as well as modern engineers explained the collapse of the Schoharie Creek Bridge.

In fact, modern engineers acted quickly and smartly by closing Mill Point Bridge, three miles downstream from the ruined Schoharie Bridge for fear the second bridge would also collapse. To help us understand our partnership with God, ask a couple of silly questions about the engineers' decision: Why bother closing the second bridge if the ten people who died in the first collapse died by the will of God? Why bother if the ones who managed to stop at the brink were saved by the favor of God? Absurd questions! Of course, engineers "bothered" because they needed to act quickly and responsibly to preserve the lives of other motorists.

Jesus, the greatest believer in God that ever lived, would clearly agree with the engineers' decision. He certainly wouldn't condemn their decision as lacking faith in God. In anecdotes like "The Good Samaritan," Jesus taught us that it's God's will for all of us to take responsibility for our neighbors. So the modern engineers did well, and as it turned out, Mill Point Bridge did collapse. Because it had been closed so quickly, no one was hurt. Whether they knew it or not, whether they believed in God or not, the engineers did God's will in protecting their neighbors. The point is, Jesus taught us to stop trying to spy out the mysterious will of God in who lives and dies. Rather, we need to get busy. We will find the Lord's will in a godly and responsible response to the ebb and flow of life's ordeals.

Not only did Jesus deny that survivors of the Siloam Tower disaster should think of themselves as less guilty (or more favored) than the dead. He goes on to tell the "commentators" of his day, *"But unless you repent, you too will all perish."** To *repent* means to change one's mind about the Lord and life. Jesus was telling the people neither to equate bad luck to the judgment of God nor good luck to the favor of God. But he had more to say. If we *are* to have the favor of the Lord, it will be the result of repenting, turning our minds and lives to the business of doing the Lord's will. Jesus makes us responsible for doing God's will.

Jesus' commentary on the collapse of the Siloam Tower was not his only commentary of this sort. He also commented on an act of brutality that Pontius Pilate, the Roman governor, ordered against some Galilean worshippers: *"Do you think that these Galileans were worse sinners than all the other Galileans because they suffered this way? I tell you, no! But unless you repent, you too will all perish."†* Pilate's brutality was an example of injustice rather than accident.

---

* Luke 13:5.
† Luke 13:1-3.

Jesus was saying that such an act of injustice in no way indicated the Lord was out to get the sufferers. Jesus also referred to *all the other Galileans*, all of whom had escaped Pilate's wrath. His point was that the survivors should not think of themselves as especially innocent or favored by the Lord. Jesus told them that they, too, needed to turn to the Lord: *"Unless you repent, you too will all perish."* The last thing lucky people should do is get cocky about having a lock on God's favor because their luck has nothing to do with being favored.

In a third case, Jesus' disciples questioned him about a blind man, *"Rabbi, who sinned, this man or his parents, that he was born blind?"** Jesus' answer is consistent with his comments on Pilate's brutality toward the Galilean worshipers and the sad deaths that resulted from the Siloam Tower collapse: *"Neither this man nor his parents sinned, but this happened so that the work of God might be displayed in his life."†* Jesus emphatically denied the cause of the blindness was sin and God's punishment for sin. He preferred to identify the awesome opportunity for God to demonstrate his power in response to the sad state of the blind man.

Again, let's turn Jesus' response around and point it at the lucky majority instead of the unfortunate man. In other words, what does Jesus' denial of sin in the case of the blind man say about those who were able to see? Certainly, none of the seeing people could claim his sight was a result of his sinlessness or some special favor he had with God. Nevertheless, any of the people in Jesus' hearing could, in fact, receive the favor of God if they would change their minds about life and the Lord. Thankfully, the potential remains for all people to experience God's work in their lives.

Jesus' comments on the situations that were current during his time, whether illnesses like blindness, injustices like

---

* John 9:2.
† John 9:3.

brutality, or accidents like a tower collapsing, were consistently down-to-earth. In other words, he did not go looking for the will of heaven above in order to assign causes to such common human ordeals. Rather, Jesus consistently pointed to the "What now?" here on earth. Someone is sick. What now? Someone has committed a crime or been the victim of a crime. What now? A terrible accident has occurred. What now? When it came to common sickness, injustice, and accident, he didn't focus on heavenly causes or scripts. He focused on the from-now-on responses. He denied being able to find God's punishments (or rewards!) in the troublesome events. He repeatedly encouraged the same response: making sure we, in the here and now, have turned our minds and lives to the task of doing the Lord's will.

Jesus categorically opposed an idea that is widespread among Christians today, that Christ's followers need only to accept, with good faith, whatever happens. In other words we only have to believe that whatever happens—easy or hard, good or evil, painful or pleasant—is God's good will. Our only responsibility is to retain an unquestioning, happy, calm outlook no matter what happens. We are the stars of God's action-adventure movies.[*] Somehow, in the end, we will dodge every bullet, climb out of every car crash, and stride into the sunset. The idea that we are living scripted lives has dulled many a Christian's sense of personal responsibility as they become fatalistic about God's will. It's a comfortable faith, but it's not a biblical faith. Jesus, as well as the Bible as a whole, consistently encourages us to search for and fight to do God's will.

Collaborating with the Lord to write the stories of our lives is dynamic because it's collaboration between living, anxious, truly free people and an insistent but respectful and responsive Lord. The dynamic nature of God's partnership with us is why the title of this book refers to the *curious*

---

[*] Thanks, Diane Knack!

partnership of God and man. Even though God is all-powerful and able to direct any event in this world as he desires, it's also entirely up to us to want a partnership with him, seek it, work for it, and hold on to it. It's not our birthright. It's not our irresistible destiny. Praise the Lord, it's available! The most reliable part of the collaboration is the Lord himself. He abides faithfully and eternally committed to his loving intentions. It's we who remain "question marks."

It's a good time to review, chapter by chapter, some of the points in this book about the Lord's curious partnership with us. The first section of the book describes the freedom upon which God has founded his creation. In this section we see that we cannot assume God's will is always being done. We have to choose his will over our own. The Lord allows us to be free because his project of love can be built on no other foundation than freedom. Freedom is a condition with which God himself must live.

Next come a number of points about God's providential care for us. The intervention of God in the lives of human beings is only visible because it stands out in relief from a world usually governed by the laws of nature and chance. We need to take advantage of the opportunity God has provided us with life by yielding to his wisdom and working with him.

Another section of the book is about dealing with trouble. When we are in trouble, the Lord can intervene in our lives and will intervene more if we ask. On the other hand, the Lord is not as likely to play favorites as we may have thought, so life is sometimes an ordeal, even for his servants. The Lord may not always keep us out of trouble, but he can help us in tangible ways if we turn to him in our trouble. Importantly, we also see that the Lord's great spiritual power can free us from our sinful, animal nature and the havoc that sinfulness wreaks in our lives.

The last section considers a number of ways that the will of God may play out in our lives. We see that even though the Lord has a wonderful plan in mind for us, we may induce a change in his plans. Surely our best future is with the Lord. God, in his graciousness, may also give us a second chance at doing his will, or, as a sign of a real relationship, he may wait for us while we lag. Sometimes the opportunity to do the Lord's "Plan A" for our lives may be lost forever, but in his love and care for us, he may provide us with a wonderful "Plan B."

In each of these chapters, at about this point in the chapter, we turned to a story about one of my friends. We won't do that here as the book ends. Instead, I now ask you to become one of our friends, not only mine, but Nila's and Brother Bob's, Linda's, Dan and Jenny's, and all the rest. You have a chance to help write your own story by collaborating with the Lord. How will your story turn out? Natural laws will determine some of your story, chance will determine some details, and you get to have some say, too. Are you concerned that the Lord will intervene as well?

The Lord is not the super CEO on the top floor of the company high-rise with an elevator to which he has the only key. If the CEO image is one of lofty power and intelligence, the Lord has the power and the wisdom. But the comparison fails miserably because it leaves out the Lord's personal knowledge of and care for each of us.

In contrast to the impersonal CEO, the Father has beheld our needy state and sent his Son down here to save us. Indeed, Jesus Christ's life on this earth is the central event of the faith, of history, and of life. God's arrival in this world, in the person of Jesus, makes Christianity unique among the religions of the world. In all the other religions, man must seek out God. Seekers build breath-taking temples, make arduous journeys, erect altars, perform rites, study books, and obey rigorous disciplines in search of God. But in Christianity, while the believer certainly should seek the Lord, Jesus reveals the Lord in search of us. Jesus expresses the priority of God's

work this way: *"You did not choose me, but I chose you."*[*]
Another verse says, *We love because he first loved us.*[†]

God sent his Son to us because we couldn't attain a relationship with him by our virtues alone. This Son died by crucifixion at a place called Golgotha, meaning Skull Hill. When his hands, feet, and side were pierced the blood flowed. Jesus didn't pop like a balloon and fly away. When he died on Skull Hill, his friends had to negotiate with Pilate for his body, unfasten the nails that held his flesh on the cross, and gingerly and reverently ease it down.

Jesus' friends had to confront his death in the rawest of conditions. They couldn't hire an undertaker to care for the remains of Jesus. They wrapped his cold body in cloths and spices, as was their custom. They also wrapped his face because they weren't just putting him to bed. He was really dead. They rolled a stone over the mouth of the sepulcher because he was really dead. It felt like a crushing defeat. This horrible death of God's Son measures the length to which God has gone in his search of a relationship with us.

The Bible says, *God demonstrates his own love for us in this: While we were still sinners, Christ died for us.*[‡] Jesus didn't rehabilitate us before he died for us. He didn't challenge us to climb the heights of personal nobility and virtue before he opened heaven's gates to us. We didn't appear innocent and adorable to him so that he pined over us like a child in a song wondering how much is that puppy in the window. On the contrary, Jesus, God's own son, surrendered his life as an atoning sacrifice for the weak and the offensive. He is that committed to his plan of love. Now it only remains for us to embrace his salvation with working, responsible faith.

If we take a humble view of our circumstances, we can hardly deny the force of chance. Most adults can look back at

---

[*] John 15:16.
[†] 1 John 4:19.
[‡] Romans 5:8.

their lives at any given point and see times when they had a brush with death. Or they may be able to think of times when they narrowly escaped financial ruin or an emotional nightmare. Like a soldier who witnesses the buddies to his right and left killed, any of us may be left to wonder what powers "chose us to survive."

Or we may wonder why we Americans were born into such a rich and safe country instead of into a third world country like the majority of people in this world whose survival is a daily ordeal. When some people seem to get more than their share of blessings or less than their share, my mother's maxim—Life isn't fair. Get over it!—doesn't quite explain.

Many of us can also look back on a good decision, the blessed result of which was totally unforeseen, so it's more like a happy accident than a sage decision on our part. Maybe it was the decision to marry, made when we were young and didn't really know what we were doing. Or we may have fallen into a challenging and fulfilling job, befriended a kind and supportive neighbor, bought a beautiful plot of land, or taken a life-changing trip. The windows of heaven seemed to open with some lucky decisions, and down flowed the blessing. Most of us are equally disappointed how some of our decisions turned out. Where is the sense in it all?

Unthinkable multitudes of events have gone before us to bring us to this moment, some we chose and most we did not. The story of our lives starts ages ago and passes through our entire line of ancestors, through the entire history of the human race, through the changes good and bad that this earth has experienced, all finally funneling down to this speck of time. Still, the greatest decision of our lives doesn't have to be left to luck. The greatest decision of our lives can be informed, purposeful, and resolute.

The Bible says, *Now is the time of God's favor.** In this very moment, this *now*, you have a choice. If you

---

* 1 Corinthians 6:2.

procrastinate, even that delay is itself a choice. The Lord says, *"I have set before you life and death, blessing and cursing: therefore choose life."**

The life the Lord promises us is the resurrection life that only he may grant when we decide to surrender our will to his. A spiritual empowerment comes with this decision of faith. It's precisely the same power the Father demonstrated when he raised Jesus out of his grave after three dark days. The Lord does not intend to simply come behind us and clean up the mess we make. He doesn't only promise forgiveness through the atoning sacrifice of Jesus on the cross. He also promises collaboration. The Bible describes believers *whose weakness was turned to strength; and who became powerful in battle.*† He will work with us to help us live the way he wants us to live. As much as Jesus' grave was open and empty on the third day after his death, we have a promise from God of eternal life.

In sharing the good news of salvation through Christ over many decades, I have found that the most common reason people balk at the invitation to turn to Jesus is the fear of failure. People just don't imagine themselves living a proper Christian life. It's not that they don't want to. They simply don't see themselves as being able to. This is where God's partnership comes in. The story of our lives can make such a dramatic turn if we will only work with the Lord from here on out.

In nearly every chapter of this book one of my friends comes to a critical moment in prayer, and many of these times could serve as good models for you now. Nila prayed, "Have your way, this time, Lord." Scott dropped to his knees, "Jesus! Save me, Jesus!" David asked the Lord to liberate him from his pride. Janis asked the Lord to show her his plan. Mike pleaded for a second chance. While I would never want to

---

* Deuteronomy 30:19.
† Hebrews 11:34.

suggest coming to Christ is as ordinary as a few words in prayer, the longest journey begins with a first step, and praying is a good first step. Because of a critical moment of prayer, the Almighty can intervene in your life to create tangible peace, health, and purpose. Our circle of friends will grow ever larger as other needy souls pray like we did, and we now invite you in.

# Acknowledgments

The subjects of each chapter, one to as many as four people, read the chapter about themselves, and most of these friends not only checked my writing for historical accuracy. They also could see much better where I was headed with their life stories by then, so they usually offered some more important and colorful details. Most of them were also so good as to offer valuable editorial comments. In keeping with the practice in the text, we will leave their last names a mystery. Other reviewers were also of immeasurable help including Tony and Janet Gray, Diane Knack, Gene Bailey, Jo Nelson, John Sanders, and Walter Brueggemann. Special thanks go to Ed Knack for his comments on the formatting of the book and to Josiah Ludovico for his cover design. Thanks to Pricilla Keim for taking the cover photo of myself. Rueben Connor served the *Not Even God* effort with utter professionalism as he designed the book's web site. Several members of my family gave moral support as well as helpful editorial comments, including Victor Rocine, Isaiah Rocine, and Bethany Rocine. I could never have written this book without the encouragement and counsel of my wife Cathy. All these friends have done their best to keep me honest and keep me from saying something silly. If I have erred, it's my own fault.

Printed in the United States
204571BV00003B/1-147/P

9 780982 070208